LEGAL DIMENSIONS OF DRUG ABUSE IN THE UNITED STATES

This comparative study of the drug abuse laws in the United States reflects some of the problems inherent in the enactment of dangerous drug laws. More important, however, it reflects the need for additional research by all individuals concerned with legislative efforts to control the indiscriminate use of narcotics, hallucinogens, stimulants, depressants and other dangerous drugs.

Drugs are purportedly classified for purposes of imposing penalties proportionate to the dangers of controlled substances. Legislative classifications differ greatly from pharmacological classifications and there is little uniformity in classification among the states. The reader is encouraged to compare the described offenses in the varied jurisdictions and take cognizance of the disparities in penalties imposed for these offenses.

The classification disparities noted above are highlighted throughout the text for purposes of encouraging the reader to review the charts presented and possibly pinpoint some of the problems inherent in the enactment of dangerous drug laws. These contrasting classification patterns indicate to the reader that: pharmacological qualities of dangerous drugs and their described effects have not been uniformly established; legislators do not take sufficient cognizance of essential pharmacological qualities of controlled substances; and pharmacological considerations are possibly pre-empted by social and economic forces such as public sentiment and lobbying activities which influence the enactment of dangerous drug laws.

LEGAL DIMENSIONS OF DRUG ABUSE IN THE UNITED STATES

CRIMINAL LAW EDUCATION
AND
RESEARCH CENTER

Publications of the Criminal Law
Education and Research Center

Volume 7

New York University
School of Law

Legal Dimensions Of Drug Abuse in The United States

By

HARVEY R. LEVINE

Assistant Professor of Law at the
University of San Diego
Former Senior Fellow,
Criminal Law Education and Research Center
New York University

CHARLES C THOMAS · PUBLISHER

Springfield · Illinois · U.S.A.

Published and Distributed Throughout the World by
CHARLES C THOMAS • PUBLISHER
Bannerstone House
301-327 East Lawrence Avenue, Springfield, Illinois, U.S.A.

© *1974, by* CHARLES C THOMAS • PUBLISHER
ISBN 0-398-02876-1
Library of Congress Catalog Card Number: 73-5545

*With THOMAS BOOKS careful attention is given to all details of
manufacturing and design. It is the Publisher's desire to present books that
are satisfactory as to their physical qualities and artistic possibilities and
appropriate for their particular use. THOMAS BOOKS will be true to those
laws of quality that assure a good name and good will.*

Printed in the United States of America
C-1

Library of Congress Cataloging in Publication Data

Levine, Harvey R.
  Legal dimensions of drug abuse in the United States.

  (New York University. Criminal Law Education and
Research Center. Monograph series, v. 7)
    1. Narcotic laws—United States. 2. Drugs—Laws
and legislation—United States. 3 Narcotic addicts—
Legal status, laws, etc—United States. I. Title.
II. Series. [DNLM: 1. Drug abuse—Legisation—U. S.
WM270 L667L 1973]
KF3890.L45   344′.73′04463   73-5545
ISBN 0-398-02876-1

Advisory Board
of the
Criminal Law Education and Research Center

CONTENTS

Chapter   *Page*

   I. INTRODUCTORY NOTE   3

  II. DEFINITIONS AND CLASSIFICATIONS CONTEMPLATED BY DRUG
      ABUSE LAWS 11

 III. FEDERAL LAW AIMED AT CONTROLLING DRUG ABUSE . . . 19

  IV. STATE DRUG ABUSE LAWS 38

   V. PRESENT TRENDS REFLECTING INCREASED UTILIZATION OF THE
      UNIFORM CONTROLLED SUBSTANCES ACT 169

  VI. THE ENFORCEMENT OF DANGEROUS DRUG LAWS: A CON-
      SIDERATION OF EXCLUSIONARY RULES OF EVIDENCE AND THE
      DEFENSE OF ENTRAPMENT 173

 VII. CIVIL COMMITMENT OF DRUG ADDICTS 186

Index 191

LEGAL DIMENSIONS OF DRUG ABUSE
IN THE UNITED STATES

To obtain a complete view of the legal dimensions of drug abuse in the United States, it is suggested that in reviewing these charts the reader compare:

>   the varied definitions and classifications of drugs with a potential for abuse;

>   the distinctions of described offenses; and

>   the diverse penalties imposed for similar offenses.

The severity of the penalties imposed reflects the legislative effort of a particular jurisdiction to deter the distribution and use of a specific dangerous drug. The reader should also take note that more significant than the distinction in types of described offenses, however, are the existing differences in the penalties imposed for similar offenses in varied jurisdictions.

This study also considers the effects of drug legislation from an enforcement perspective and includes a brief description of some judicial ramifications essential in evaluating the efficacy of dangerous drug legislation. The complex federal classification of controlled substances is also discussed at length in the section which focuses on federal law.

Considering the legal dimensions of drug abuse from these perspectives will illuminate the increased need for effectively coordinated efforts among legislators, judges, law enforcement agents, pharmacological experts, behavioral scientists and educators. These synthesized efforts are essential to establishing a realistic, effective, meaningful approach to solving some of the problems of dangerous drug abuse in America.

YOU MAY ALSO BE INTERESTED IN . . .

CHARLES C THOMAS • PUBLISHER • SPRINGFIELD • ILLINOIS

LEGAL DIMENSIONS OF DRUG ABUSE IN THE UNITED STATES

Chapter I

INTRODUCTORY NOTE

A. Prefatory Note

THE AMERICAN dangerous drug laws presented within this study cannot represent a completely accurate status of the law. American dangerous drug laws are constantly being amended in an effort to curb the growing wave of drug abuse. However, a study of the legal dimensions of drug abuse in the United States does have significant value even if many of the laws have been amended by the time the materials are published.

A comparative study of the drug abuse laws reflects some of the legislative problems which arise. The juxtaposition of the drug laws of the fifty states and the federal government indicate significant trends and reflect inconsistencies which are invaluable in evaluating existing legislation.

More important, the comparative study reflects the need for additional research by all individuals concerned with legislative efforts to control the indiscriminate use of narcotics, hallucinogens, stimulants, depressants and other dangerous drugs. This study further illustrates the need for a combined, coordinated and concentrated effort directed at reconciling existing legislative contradictions and inconsistencies. Coordinated research activities should be directed at formulating model criteria to be used in the enactment of dangerous drug laws.

The legal dimensions of drug abuse include a portrayal of the status of the dangerous drug laws of the United States. The legislative "sketches" indicate the increasing trend toward classifying drugs that have a potential for abuse. The legislative definitions and classifications are ordinarily followed by statutes which describe offenses and set forth penalties. The contrast of definitions and classifications of dangerous drugs provided the foundation for this study. The varied approaches to legislative definitions and classifications are partially responsible for the dis-

3

parities in the penalties imposed for the illegal sale and use of drugs with a potential for abuse.

B. A Comparison of Legislative Definitions and Classifications

The purpose of classifying drugs should be to impose penalties proportionate to the inherent dangers of the controlled substances. Legislative classifications differ greatly from pharmacological classifications and there is little uniformity in classifications among the states. With some exceptions most statutes define and classify dangerous drugs into one of the following three categories:

1. narcotics
2. hallucinogens, and
3. dangerous drugs (stimulants and depressants such as amphetamines and barbiturates).

These categories are usually established for purposes of providing contrasting penalties for offenses involving the drugs within any respective category. The penalties for offenses involving narcotic drugs are usually most severe; penalties imposed for offenses involving the dangerous drugs (usually amphetamine and barbiturate-type drugs) are least severe. However, there are significant differences in the statutory approaches to the classification of particular controlled substances.

The most significant classification disparities are reflected by the statutes prohibiting the sale or possession of marihuana. Thirteen states define and classify marihuana as a narcotic drug, and it is consequently grouped with the opiates such as morphine and heroin. The other 37 states and the federal government have classified marihuana as an hallucinogenic substance. What difference does it make if marihuana is defined as a narcotic or an hallucinogen? The distinction gathers significance when we consider the penalties which are imposed for offenses involving substances defined or classified as narcotics or hallucinogens. For example, the Texas statute defines marihuana as a narcotic drug. A first offense involving possession of this "narcotic" substance is punishable by two years to life imprisonment. In the neighboring state of New Mexico, marihuana is not defined or classified as a

narcotic drug and a first offense involving the possession of marihuana is punished as a misdemeanor with a maximum of six
months imprisonment and/or a fine of $100. It is apparent that
the penalties which are imposed often depend upon the definition and classification of a particular controlled substance.

The study also indicated that legislative classification discrep-
ancies extended to areas involving "hard drugs" traditionally
recognized as having addiction forming and addiction sustaining
qualities. Cocaine is defined and classified as a narcotic drug and
consequently grouped with the opiates by 49 states and the federal government. However in Wisconsin, cocaine is defined and
classified as a dangerous drug, not a narcotic drug. Again, this
gathers particular significance when we consider the fact that in
Wisconsin penal sanctions for offenses involving narcotic drugs
are more severe than for offenses involving controlled substances
classified as dangerous drugs.

The legislative definitions and classifications of drugs traditionally classified and grouped as hallucinogenic substances such
as LSD, peyote, psilocybin and mescaline further illustrate some
of the contrasting statutory concepts. Most states group LSD,
peyote, psilocybin, mescaline and other drugs having a tendency
to create bizarre perceptual images as hallucinogenic substances
and offenses involving these drugs are punished accordingly.
However, it is most significant to note that Massachusetts, Rhode
Island and South Carolina define and classify these same drugs
as narcotics. This invariably implies that in these three states
these drugs are considered to have addiction forming and addiction sustaining characteristics similar to the more commonly accepted narcotic drugs such as heroin and other opiates. In contrast, in an effort to control the abuse of LSD, Georgia statutes
do not define or classify LSD as an hallucinogen or a narcotic
drug. The drug is listed separately for purposes of prohibiting
the illegal sale or possession of this drug and, therefore, the
Georgia statute avoided falling prey to the dilemma created by
legislative groupings of harmful drugs. It should also be noted
that the laws of Alaska group the hallucinogens with the stimulant and depressant drugs. In Indiana all non-narcotic drugs with

a potential for abuse are classified together. Therefore, from a punishment perspective the Indiana statutes treat offenses involving LSD, amphetamines and barbiturates similarly.

The classification disparities noted above are highlighted for purposes of encouraging the reader to review the charts presented below and possibly pinpoint some of the problems inherent in the enactment of dangerous drug laws.

The contrasting statutory classification patterns indicate that:

1. pharmacological qualities of dangerous drugs and their described effects have not been uniformly established;
2. legislators do not take sufficient cognizance of essential pharmacological qualities of controlled substances; and

TABLE I—CONTRASTING PHARMACOLOGICAL AND
LEGISLATIVE VIEWS

Type of Drug	Pharmacological Criteria (Harmful Effects)	Legislative Views (Penal Sanctions)
Narcotics (Heroin and Morphine)	High addiction forming and addiction sustaining liabilities (does not include marihuana)	Most severe penalties (Most states still include marihuana in the "narcotic" group.)
Hallucinogens (LSD, Peyote, Psilocybin, Mescaline)	Psychological dependence can develop but there is no tolerance which leads to physical addiction as with narcotics. (Trend at Federal and state levels indicates marihuana is increasingly being classified as an hallucinogen.)	Penalties are generally much less harsh than those imposed for offenses involving narcotics.
Depressants (Barbiturates)	*Often lead to tolerance and physical addiction.* There is substantial evidence that barbiturates are cumulatively more dangerous than the opiates. Where a state of addiction is reached abstinence effects are even more severe than those attributable to opiate withdrawal.	*Penalties are least severe.* Most states punish unlawful possession as a misdemeanor and unlawful sales are punished much less harshly than offenses involving narcotics or hallucinogens.
Stimulants (Amphetamines)	No physical dependence develops but they often precipitate agressive behavior often implicated in assaultive acts.	Penalties are almost always similar to those for offenses involving barbiturates.

3. pharmacological criteria are often pre-empted by social and economic forces such as public sentiment and lobbying activities which influence the enactment of dangerous drug laws.

Table I reflects the sharp contrast between pharmacologically defined dangers and statutory penalties imposed for offenses involving controlled substances.

The *Federal Drug Abuse Prevention and Control Act of 1970* reflects the growing importance of legislative classification of drugs having a potential for abuse. The complex federal classification of controlled substances is discussed at length in the section of this study discussing federal law. The importance of these classification efforts cannot be over-emphasized, when we consider that, with slight modifications, the comprehensive federal controlled substance groupings have been adopted by Idaho, Louisiana, Maryland, Mississippi, New Jersey, North Dakota, South Dakota, Utah, Virginia, West Virginia and Wyoming. Undoubtedly, these categories of harmful substances will be recognized and adopted by many other jurisdictions.

3. Offenses and Penalties: Jurisdictional Comparisons

In an effort to control the unlawful manufacture, distribution, sale or possession of drugs with a potential for abuse, each state and the federal government impose penalties for these offenses. The severity of the penalties imposed reflect the attitude of the particular jurisdiction toward specific offenses and particular drugs. The reader is, therefore, advised to compare the described offenses in the varied jurisdictions. The disparity in the penalties imposed for these offenses is partially explained by the existing classification distinctions among the states.

There are certain offenses which are punished more severely than others. Most vigorous efforts have been directed toward preventing the sale of narcotics to minors. In Alaska anyone who provides information which leads to the arrest and conviction of another unlawfully selling narcotic drugs to a minor is eligible for a reward of $1,000. Oklahoma provides for a possible sentence of death in the electric chair for selling narcotic drugs to minors. Alabama, Missouri and Texas also have statutes which provide for death sentences for these offenses. Federal law provides for twice the penalty imposed for the distribution of narcotic drugs if the distribution is to a minor. In sharp contrast, it should be noted that Georgia, Indiana and Kansas statutes do not have specific provisions prohibiting the sale of a narcotic drug to a minor. In these jurisdictions the sale to minors is punished as a sale to any other individual.

The reader should also take cognizance of other described offenses which are directed at the control of drug abuse. For example, one of the most significant provisions of the *Federal Drug Abuse Prevention and Control Act of 1970* is directed at controlling the sale of drugs by organized crime. This poignant provision provides harsh penalties to persons engaged in the "continuing criminal enterprise" of distributing controlled substances.

More significant than the distinction in types of described offenses are the existing differences in the penalties imposed for similar offenses. Note, for example, that in Nebraska the first offense involving the possession of marijuana is punishable by imprisonment in the county jail for seven days. In sharp contrast, *the same offense,* if occurring in the state of Texas is punishable by a maximum sentence of life imprisonment. The variations in penalties extend to all other drugs with a potential for abuse. In Alabama, for example, the punishments for offenses involving amphetamines and barbiturates are less severe than the penalties imposed for offenses involving other controlled substances. Compare this to Iowa where harsher penalties are imposed for the unlawful manufacture, distribution, sale or possession of amphetamines and barbiturates than for similar offenses involving other drugs with a potential for abuse.

The jurisdictions have enacted varied penalties imposed upon first offenders charged with unlawful possession of drugs with a potential for abuse. Note that under federal law, the first offender charged with unlawful possession may have criminal charges conditionally discharged upon satisfactory compliance with probationary terms. Furthermore, minors who are first offenders, have the opportunity to have their criminal records, including records of arrest, expunged upon satisfactory compliance with probationary conditions. However, it will be noted that the philosophy of "one more chance" is not adopted by many of the states which have adopted the federal classifications in the form of the *Uniform Controlled Substances Act.* Although Maryland and New Jersey have adopted the conditional discharge and expungement features of the federal law, Virginia, in adopting the federal classifications, did not adopt the conditional discharge and expungement provisions. Other states such as North Dakota, South Dakota and West Virginia, in adopting the *Uniform Controlled Substances Act,* provide for conditional discharge of first offender possession offenses, but the provisions relating to expungement of criminal records are not adopted.

At this point, it is clearly evident that a comparison of the dangerous drug laws in the United States illuminates some of the problems inherent in the enactment of laws aimed at controlling drug abuse.

The study also considers the efficacy of legislation from an enforcement perspective. An evaluation of the dangerous drug laws and the enforcement of these laws should not be divorced from considerations of constitutional dimensions as interpreted by the courts. The courts delicately balance constitutional guarantees with the need for enforcement of dangerous drug laws. This study, therefore, includes a very brief description of some judicial ramifications essential in evaluating the efficacy of dangerous drug legislation. The doctrines relating to the exclusionary rules of evidence and the defense of entrapment are briefly considered for purposes of illustrating the increased need to coordinate the activities of legislators, judges and law enforcement agents when considering the enactment of dangerous drug laws.

In an effort to emphasize the growing importance of drug addict rehabilitation perspectives the federal law relating to the civil commitment of narcotic addicts is briefly discussed. Many states have enacted civil commitment programs and these trends must be recognized when considering the legal dimensions of drug abuse.

To obtain a complete view of the legal dimensions of drug abuse in the United States, it is suggested that in reviewing the material which follows, the reader compare:

1. the varied definitions and classifications of drugs with a
   potential for abuse;
2. the distinctions of described offenses; and
3. the diverse penalties imposed for similar offenses.

Considering the legal dimensions of drug abuse from these
perspectives will illuminate the increased need for effectively coordinated efforts among legislators, judges, law enforcement
agents, pharmacological experts, behavioral scientists and educators. These synthesized efforts are essential to the control of drug
abuse in America.

Chapter II

DEFINITIONS AND CLASSIFICATIONS CONTEMPLATED BY DRUG ABUSE LAWS

THE SUBSTANCES which often lead to abuse have become known as "controlled drugs." These drugs are defined and classified for purposes of enacting legislation which imposes legal restraints on the manufacture, sale, distribution or possession of these substances. The *Federal Comprehensive Drug Abuse Prevention and Control Act of 1970* reflects the increasing significance of properly classifying drugs which are liable to be abused.

Some definitions and classifications which have been helpful in formulating the criminal laws relating to drug abuse are presented below. The controlled substances presently fall into three broad categories: narcotics, hallucinogens and dangerous drugs. Narcotics have generally included the opiates and in some cases marihuana. The dangerous drugs have included stimulants (the most often abused being amphetamines) and depressants (the most often abused being barbiturates). The hallucinogens include LSD, peyote and mescaline.

A. Narcotics

For legal purposes a narcotic does not refer to a specific class of drugs chemically similar or having similar pharmacological effects. In the eyes of the law, the term *narcotic* embraces varied classes of drugs that have been similarly classified for the purposes of legal regulation. This is best illustrated by the fact that under most state laws marijuana is classified as a narcotic. However, there are some states where marihuana offenses are treated under separate statutory classifications. Arizona is an example of this classification approach.

1. Opiates

The opiates are considered a narcotic drug. Opium, morphine, and their compounds and derivatives and the synthetic equivalents comprise the opiates. These drugs are of substantial medical

11

value. The most common are morphine which is used for the relief of pain, and codeine which is used for the relief of cough.

The opiate which is the chief drug of addiction in the United States is heroin, which is a derivative of morphine. Heroin has been described as a depressant which mitigates anxiety and lessens the primary drives such as sex and hunger. Repeated and lengthened use of heroin leads to a tolerance for the drug and physical dependence. An overdose of this narcotic drug will often result in respiratory failure and death. Withdrawing from the use of heroin involves muscle aches, cramps and nausea which reaches its most severe point 24 to 48 hours after withdrawal.

Unlike many of the other narcotic substances, heroin is a totally illegal drug in view of the fact that it cannot be lawfully imported or manufactured under any circumstances. It is not used in the practice of medicine the way other opiates such as morphine and codeine are. Consequently, all the heroin which is available to the American user is smuggled into the country. The Middle East is often the source of the illegal heroin supply in the United States. The sale or distribution of heroin or the possession of heroin *under all circumstances* is illegal. Although it does not differ substantially from the morphine from which it is derived, it is classified as totally illegal because of its luring effect to those who experience the euphoria associated with the use of the drug resulting from relief of chronic anxiety. Another reason for a total ban on the drug is because it presently serves no known medical purpose. The opiates are derived from the opium poppy. The countries which produce opium for subsequent conversion for medical purposes are Argentina, Bulgaria, Czechoslovakia, Germany, France, Hungary, Norway, Poland, Romania, USSR, Turkey, Burma, India, Japan, Pakistan, and Australia. The United States is not a country which produces opium. It imports all of the opiates which are used for medical purposes.

2. Cocaine

Cocaine is another drug which is included in many statutory definitions as a narcotic. It is a derivative of the leaves of the coca plant which is cultivated in various parts of South America. The most prevalent sources are Bolivia, Colombia and Peru.

Some authorities state that cocaine does not create tolerance or physical dependence whereas others assert that it does. The drug is not considered addicting because there is no evidence of physiological withdrawal symptoms. The coca leaves are chewed but the derivatives (prepared coca and cocaine) are often sniffed, injected, chewed, smoked, or rubbed into the mucosa.

Cocaine reactions vary from central nervous system irritability and possible convulsions, to death if taken in large doses. Those who become chronic sniffers of cocaine often develop nasal ulcerations. In medical practice cocaine is used as a local anaesthetic.

3. Marihuana

The technical or scientific name for the plant is *cannabis indica* or *cannabis sativa*. It is a derivative of the flowering tops of the female hemp plant. The plant is often found growing wild or it may be cultivated in almost any area of the globe. After it is introduced to many areas it continues to grow wild. Depending on the soil and the degree of cultivation, this weed-like annual plant may reach a height of from one to 20 feet. It is useful as a source of fiber seed and the narcotic resin which is the basis of its use, is an intoxicant. The resinous content of the plant varies widely with the climate and the quality of the soil. This may partially explain some of the widely differing reports of the reactions and effects of the drug in different parts of the world and in varied studies.

Cannabinol, the resin of the cannabis plant which is responsible for its potency as an intoxicating drug, is extracted from cultivated plants in relatively pure form. It is known as *charas* in India and used for smoking or eating. Hashish is a powdered and sifted form of this resin. A less potent preparation is made from the cut tops of the uncultivated female plant. The less potent preparation has a relatively low content of resin, which is known as *bhang*. Marihuana is the Mexican name for *bhang*.

The hemp plant was cultivated for its fiber and was one of the earliest crops of the American colonies reported here as early as 1632. In Kentucky the first crop was planted in 1775, and it was responsible for a major source of income there for many years. There is no indication of drug traffic developing in the early colonies. The smoking of marihuana did not become prevalent in the United States until about 1910, when it began to evolve from Mexico.

Professor Roger Adams at the University of Illinois has produced a synthetic substance referred to as *pyrahexyl* compound which is substantially similar to the active ingredient of *cannabis indica.*

The physical effects of cannabis intoxication are raised pulse rate and blood pressure, dilated, sluggish pupils, injected conjunctival vessels, tremor of tongue and mouth, cold extremities, rapid shallow breathing, ataxia and active deep reflexes. The severity of these symptoms will depend upon the amount of the resin-like material contained in the preparation and upon the individual.

The psychological effects of the drug vary greatly. Some of the reported effects have included euphoria, excitement, disturbed associations, changes in the appreciation of time and space, raised auditory sensibility, emotional upheaval, illusions and hallucinations. It is a matter of present controversy whether or not there are any aphrodisiac effects and many argue that despite the increased consciousness of sexual fantasies there is no connection with any responsive action to these fantasies. The intoxicating effect of the drug may wear off within a few hours but may last longer in the case of a toxic dose.

B. Dangerous Drugs

State law and federal law indicate that there is a growing awareness of the need to classify drugs. Recent legislation reflects this growing awareness as is illustrated by those laws which punish the possession or sale of those substances classified as *narcotic drugs* differently from the punishment for the possession or sale of a substance referred to as a *dangerous drug.* Laws vary in classifying substances. Marihuana is increasingly being treated as an hallucinogenic or dangerous drug as distinguished from its earlier classification in most statutes as a narcotic. Whether a substance is classified as a narcotic or dangerous drug is usually based on studies which reflect the degree of physical dependence which is usually associated with abuse of the drug.

The classification of dangerous drugs usually refers to three categories of non-narcotic drugs that have been shown to be abused and which have a stimulant (amphetamines), depressant (barbiturates), or hallucinogenic (LSD) effect.

1. Stimulants

The technical names of the amphetamine type of stimulants are Benzedrine®, Dexedrine®, and Methedrine®. These are often referred to as "pep pills." The amphetamines are marketed in twelve different types of preparations. Medically, these drugs are used for the relief of fatigue, for people who are interested in controlling overweight, and for the treatment of mental disorders.

The effects of these drugs on the central nervous system usually include feelings of euphoria or well being, feelings of confidence, and some increase in alertness and initiative. These preparations are also known to reduce or prevent sleepiness and fatigue.

One of the outstanding effects of the drugs is to reduce appetite. For this purpose they have been prescribed in the treatment of obesity, although they are usually not recommended for this purpose, and most people who take them do so by self-prescription, which often leads to increased dosage and the result of toxic side effects. Taken orally or injected, the drugs have been abused by those who have experienced the intoxicating effects of the amphetamines when taken in larger than therapeutic doses.

Because of the tolerance that develops with the use of amphetamines, there is often an increase in the dosage. Too large a dose often results in hallucinations and bizarre mental effects. This is more likely to occur when the drug is injected intravenously in the powdered form. It is reported that physical dependence does not develop with the use of the drug.

Individuals who use amphetamines excessively sometimes alternate the use of an amphetamine with the use of a barbiturate. This effort to attain an emotional equilibrium often results in a behavior pattern which waivers from excitement to depression. The individual who becomes largely dependent upon this type of dangerous drug is exposed to the dangers of death or serious illness if an overdose of the drug is taken.

2. Depressants

The depressant drugs most often abused are the barbiturates. The barbiturates were introduced into clinical practice in 1903. They have proved to be valuable drugs, and they have been widely used with few adverse effects.

The therapeutic uses of the barbiturates are well known. They include the relief of insomnia and anxiety, the treatment of epilepsy, and the induction of anesthesia. This group of sedative and sleep-producing drugs are derived from barbituric acid. The first hypnotic barbiturate drug was prepared in 1882 under the name "barbital." Many barbiturates have been synthesized since that time and sold under a variety of chemical and proprietary names. With a few exceptions, the distinguishing feature of the names of the barbiturate drugs is that they end with the suffix "al."

Pentothal® and Amytal®, two types of barbiturates, are used intravenously; and if proper doses are administered by a skilled physician, a semi-conscious state is induced. The patients conscious inhibitions and deceptions are diminished with the result that questions may be more truthfully answered than otherwise. When used in this manner in the course of legal investigations, it is known as "truth serum." However, its efficiency is dubious, and results obtained with it are usually not acceptable to the courts. Psychiatrists often administer the drug in the course of investigations of the unconscious factors in connection with some psychiatric disorders.

There is divided opinion among medical experts as to the addictive and habit-forming potentialities of barbiturates. Some medical experts argue that barbiturates are just as addictive as are narcotics. Other experts contend that the barbiturates are not addictive but they are habit-forming. Excessive use of the drug may result in impaired judgment, loss of emotional control, loss of balance, impaired speech, and sometimes coma or death. Barbiturates are often used as a suicidal agent.

Other depressants that are a part of the drug abuse problem are some of the sedative and tranquilizing drugs which were introduced in 1950. Although they are not chemically similar to the barbiturates, they are similar in effect. Some of these are meprobamate (Miltown®, Equanil®) and chlordiazeoxide (Librium®). There are medical experts who contend that abuse of the sedatives can lead to drug intoxication and physical dependence. An overdose is often used in suicides, and there have been some reports of deaths during withdrawal.

C. Hallucinogens

Hallucinogens are those drugs which manifest their presence through the creation of bizarre mental images. These drugs are often referred to as psychedelic drugs because they produce a variety of intense and unusual psychic effects. Some of the milder hallucinogens are peyote and mescaline. The stronger hallucinogens are LSD (d-lysergic acid diethylamide) and psilocybin.

Until use developed in the modern world, peyote and mescaline were, and still are, used by Indians in both North and South America. In the 1960's the most potent of the hallucinogens became available in this country. This was LSD, discovered by Dr. Albert Hofmann in Switzerland in 1943. The drug was originally used by European psychiatrists to artificially induce psychoses under controlled conditions.

1. LSD

LSD is a tasteless, odorless, white powder prepared from ergot, a fungus growth on rye grain, or it may be produced synthetically. It appears on the illegitimate market as sugar cubes treated with LSD and more recently in capsules and tablets.

LSD users refer to experiences with LSD, which usually include vivid hallucinations in colors, as "taking a trip." Although the precise effects upon the human body are still not clearly defined, LSD has been reported to cause prolonged psychosis, homosexual impulses, suicidal inclinations and activation of previously latent psychoses.

2. *Peyote*

Peyote is an hallucinogenic substance found in some of the button-shaped growths of a small, spineless cactus which grows wild in southern Texas and Mexico. Mescaline is a natural alkaloid which grows in the same plant. Peyote and mescaline appear in capsule or liquid form or as a powder that is dissolved in water.

3. *Psilocybin*

Psilocybin is a substance derived from a mushroom fungus. It appears in either liquid or powder form. There is no evidence of physical dependence developing as a consequence of using the hallucinogens.

CHAPTER III

FEDERAL LAW AIMED AT CONTROLLING DRUG ABUSE

A. Brief History of Federal Legislation Preceding Passage of the Comprehensive Drug Abuse Prevention and Control Act of 1970

SINCE 1887, THERE have been at least fifty separate types of federal legislation which have attempted to prevent and control drug abuse in the United States. The Act of 1970 has repealed the majority of these earlier acts and has attempted to deal with the problem of drug abuse in a more comprehensive manner by combining the most advantageous elements of each of these separate acts. Some of the principal laws which have been repealed are the Harrison Narcotic Act (Sections 4701-4736 of the Internal Revenue Code of 1954), the Marihuana Tax Act (Sections 4741-4762 of the 1954 Code) the Narcotic Drug Import and Export Act (21 U.S.C. 171, 173, 174, 176-184, 185) and the Narcotics Manufacturing Act of 1960 (21 U.S.C. 501-517).

Tracing the history and development of the recently repealed federal legislation should indicate the importance of dealing with the problem of drug abuse in a comprehensive manner. More specifically, early legislation was directed at controlling abuse of narcotic drugs and was not directed toward preventing the abuse of other drugs such as many of the hallucinogenic and stimulant-depressant type substances which later became a substantial portion of the wave of drug abuse.

Prior to the first decade of the twentieth century, there was no restriction of any kind on the importation or use of opium or its derivatives in the United States. Many patent medicines contained opium or derivatives of opium without carrying any warning label, and there were many people who were physically dependent, as addicts, upon medicines which were bought and sold without restriction. Opium smoking, introduced by orientals but spreading rapidly to all classes in the United States, went on unhindered. Physicians prescribed narcotics without supervision or limitation; pharmacists, and even general storekeepers, sold narcotics without prescription. These conditions gave rise to the need for the enactment of the federal narcotic laws.

1. *Harrison Narcotic Law (originally passed in 1914 and later included in the amendments to the Internal Revenue Code, Sections 4701-4736, [1954])*

This law controlled the importation, manufacturer, processing, buying, selling, dispensing or giving away of opium, coca leaves and all their compounds, derivatives and preparations. It was in the form of a tax act and required registration and an occupational tax for all persons who dealt in these drugs. Sales or transfers of the drugs under control were made only by the use of official order forms obtained by registrants from the collector of Internal Revenue.

The Harrison Narcotic Law and the Marihuana Tax Act were primarily designed to suppress traffic in addicting drugs and were not intended to produce revenue.

2. *Narcotic Drug Import and Export Act (21 U.S.C. 171, 173, 174-184, 185)*

This act as amended was directed at limiting the importation of crude opium and coca leaves to the quantities necessary to supply medical and legitimate requirements only. Licenses were issued to three manufacturers only to import drugs for processing and resale to a larger number of pharmaceutical houses in the United States. The importation of opium was prohibited without exception. Under this act, the Surgeon General of the United States Public Health Service estimated annually the amount of narcotics required for the following year for legitimate medical and research purposes for the Commissioner of the Bureau of Narcotics.

3. *Marihuana Tax Act (Sections 4741-4762 of the 1954 Internal Revenue Code)*

This law sets up taxes and regulations concerning the importation, manufacture and trafficking in marihuana which were similar to those specified for opium and cocaine under the Harrison Narcotic Law. Since marihuana is not used medically, the enforcement of this act was one almost entirely of suppression rather than restriction and regulation of legal medical use.

4. *Narcotic Transportation Act (18 U.S.C.A. 3616)*

This law, passed in 1939 and amended in 1950, made it unlawful to use vehicles, vessels or aircraft to conceal or transport contraband drugs. The regulation provided for seizure of the means of transport if so used. Many vehicles and small boats were seized.

5. *The Opium Poppy Control Act of 1942 (21 U.S.C. 188-188n)*

This law prohibited the growth in the United States of the opium poppy except under license. Since there was no need to produce opium in the United States, no licenses were issued under the law. The law did provide penalties for any person growing the opium poppy without a license.

6. *Federal Food, Drug and Cosmetic Act of 1906*

This act, as amended, prohibits the movement in interstate commerce of adulterated and misbranded food, drugs, devices, cosmetics, etc. This act placed all drugs in two classes: those to be dispensed on prescription only and those non-prescription drugs which could be sold by druggists over the counter without prescription. This act was the legal basis for suppression for all sales of sedative drugs, particularly the barbiturates, except upon medical prescription, but flagrant violations continued because of the inadequate funds and personnel to enforce the law rigidly.

7. *Drug Abuse Control Amendments (1965)*

This act gave the Food and Drug Administration strict inventory control, from manufacturer to consumer over barbiturates, amphetamines and other drugs to be determined as dangerous. It limited the number of times a prescription could be refilled by a pharmacist and made it an offense to possess the drugs without a prescription. Other drugs which were included administratively were peyote, mescaline, LSD, DMT, psilocybin and some tranquilizers. Special penalties were provided for the sale of drugs to juveniles who for the purpose of the act were designated under age 21 instead of age 18, usually specified as the age of juveniles.

In an effort to deal with the growing wave of drug abuse, the federal government consolidated the poignant provisions of the above mentioned Acts in the *Comprehensive Drug Abuse Prevention and Control Act of 1970.*

B. Significant Provisions of the Comprehensive Drug Abuse Prevention and Control Act of 1970[1]

The act of 1970 consolidated the provisions of the previous laws and compressed the laws into one comprehensive legislative act. The act classified the controlled substances in one of five possible categories. The classification is based upon the drugs potential for abuse and its physiological and psychological effects. The penalties imposed for the offenses involving any controlled substance correspond to the schedule the regulated substance has been classified under.

1. The Schedules of Controlled Substances

Drugs which have a potential for abuse are classified according to criteria promulgated by the act. The act provides that the Attorney General shall consider the following factors with respect to each drug or substance proposed to be controlled or removed from the schedules:

(1) Its actual or relative potential for abuse.

(2) Scientific evidence of its pharmacological effect if known.

(3) The state of current scientific knowledge regarding the drug or other substances.

(4) Its history and current pattern of abuse.

(5) The scope, duration, and significance of abuse.

(6) What, if any, risk there is to the public health.

(7) Its psychic or physiological dependence liability.

---

[1] *Comprehensive Drug Abuse Prevention and Control Act of 1970,* 21 U.S.C.A. 801 et seq. (1970).

(8) Whether the substance is an immediate precursor of a substance already controlled.[2]

The criteria set forth are used as determinative factors in placing a controlled substance within any of the five schedules.

Schedule I: To be placed in this category these findings must indicate:

(a) The drug or other substance has a high potential for abuse.

(b) The drug or other substance has no currently accepted medical use in treatment in the United States.

(c) There is a lack of accepted safety for use of the drug or other substance under medical supervision.[3]

It is most significant to note that none of the drugs placed within this schedule have a currently acceptable medical use in the United States.[4] Schedule I controlled substances include: (1) 42 specific opiates;[5] (2) 22 specific opium derivatives (including heroin); and (3) 17 hallucinogenic substances (including LSD, marihuana, mescaline, peyote, psilocybin and tetrahydrocannabinols).[6]

The federal government has defined marihuana as an hallucinogenic substance. This may be compared to those states which still define marihuana as a narcotic drug.

Schedule II: To be placed in this category the findings must indicate:[7]

(a) The drug or other substance has a high potential for abuse.

(b) The drug or other substance has a currently accepted medical use in treatment in the United States or a currently accepted medical use with severe restrictions.

---

[2] 21 U.S.C.A. 811(c) (1970).

[3] 21 U.S.C.A. 812(b)(1) (1970).

[4] 21 U.S.C.A. 812(b) (1) (B) (1970).

[5] The term opiate is defined as "any drug or other substance having an addiction-forming or addiction-sustaining liability similar to morphine or being capable of conversion into a drug having such addiction-forming or addiction-sustaining liability (21 U.S.C.A. 802[17] 1970).

[6] 21 U.S.C.A. 812(a)(b)(c) (1970).

[7] 21 U.S.C.A. 812(b)(2)(A)(B)(C) (1970).

(c) Abuse of the drug or other substances may lead to severe psychological or physical dependence.

Schedule II controlled substances include 21 specific opiates.[8]

Schedule III: To be placed in this category the findings must indicate:

(a) The drug or other substance has a potential for abuse less than the drugs or other substances in Schedule I and II.

(b) The drug or other substance has a currently accepted medical use in treatment in the United States.

(c) Abuse of the drug or other substance may lead to moderate or low physical dependence or high psychological dependence.[9]

Schedule III controlled substances include the following substances having a stimulant effect upon the central nervous system:

(a) 1. Amphetamine.
2. Phenmetrazine.
3. Any substance (except an injectable liquid) which contains any quantity of methamphetamine.
4. Methylphenidate.[10]

Schedule III also includes the following controlled substances having a depressant effect on the central nervous system:

(b) 1. Any substance having any quantity of a derivative of barbituric acid.
2. Chorhexadol.
3. Glutethimide.
4. Lysergic acid.
5. Lysergic acid amide.
6. Methyprylon.
7. Phencyclidine.
8. Sulfondiethylmethane.
9. Sulfonethylmethane.
10. Sulfonmethane.[11]

(c) Nalorphine.

---

[8] 21 U.S.C.A. 812 (1970).
[9] 21 U.S.C.A. 812(b)(3)(A)(B)(C) (1970).
[10] Schedule III: 21 U.S.C.A. 812 (1970).
[11] Schedule III: 21 U.S.C.A. 812 (1970).

(d) Included within Schedule III are compounds, mixtures and preparations which contain limited quantities of any of the following narcotic drugs.[12]

Schedule IV:[13] To be placed in this category the findings must indicate:

(a) The drug or other substance has a low potential for abuse relative to the drugs or other substances in Schedule III.

(b) The drug or other substance has a currently accepted medical use in treatment in the United States.

(c) Abuse of the drug or other substance may lead to limited physical dependence or psychological dependence relative to the drugs or other substances in Schedule III.[14]

Schedule IV includes the following substances:

1. Barbital.
2. Chloral betaine.
3. Chloral hydrate.
4. Ethinamate.
5. Methohexital.
6. Meprobamate.
7. Methylphenobarbital.
8. Paraldehyde.
9. Petrichloral.
10. Phenobarbital.[15]

Schedule V:[16] To be placed in this schedule the findings must indicate:

(a) No drug or other substance has a low potential for abuse relative to the drugs or other substances in Schedule IV.

(b) The drug or other substance has a currently accepted medical use in treatment in the United States.

(c) Abuse of the drug or other substance may lead to lim-

---

[12] Schedule III: 21 U.S.C.A. 812 (1970).
[13] Schedule IV: 21 U.S.C.A. 812 (1970).
[14] 21 U.S.C.A. 812(b)(4)(A)(B)(C) (1970).
[15] Schedule IV: 21 U.S.C.A. 812 (1970).
[16] Schedule V: 21 U.S.C.A. 812 (1970).

ited physical dependence relative to the drugs or substances in Schedule IV.[17]

The drugs and substances included within this schedule are compounds, mixtures, and preparations containing limited quantities of narcotic drugs and include one or more non-narcotic active medicinal ingredients so that the mixture or preparation acquires medicinal qualities which are not possessed by the narcotic drug alone.[18]

The five schedules as appearing in the federal statute, at first glance resemble a chemistry textbook. However, the substances are classified by the use of the following criteria:[19]

(1) A major consideration is the pharmacological properties of a drug. It is vital to ascertain whether a drug has a depressant or an hallucinogenic effect.[20]

(2) A consideration of all scientific knowledge regarding the substance.[21]

(3) A comprehensive study of the patterns of abuse which would include the social, economic, and ecological characteristics of the segments of the population involved in specific drug abuse.[22]

(4) It must be determined whether the abuse is of a temporary nature or whether it is an abuse problem of chronic dimensions such as heroin addiction.[23]

(5) It must be established that the drug creates a danger to the public health.[24]

(6) A paramount consideration is whether the substance contains addiction forming or addiction sustaining liabilities at physiological and psychological levels.[25]

These considerations determine under which schedule a controlled substance will be classified. The classification of controlled substance is of paramount importance because the laws

---

[17] 21 U.S.C.A. 812(b)(5)(A)(B)(C) (1970).

[18] Schedule V: 21 U.S.C.A. 812 (1970).

[19] See generally, Pub. L. 91-513, Sec. 201, 1970 U.S. Code Cong. and Adm. News, P-5659 et seq.

[21] *Ibid.*, at 5662.

[22] *Ibid.*, at 5663.

[23] *Ibid.*

[24] *Ibid.*

[25] *Ibid.*

of the states are now adopting the federal classifications in the form of the Uniform Controlled Substances Act. The states' classifications are similar to those in the federal law with the exception of some minor modifications.[26]

2. Federal Law Requiring Registration of Manufacturers, Distributors and Dispensers of Controlled Substances

Part C of the federal law establishes rules and regulations for the registration of manufacturers, distributors, and dispensers of controlled substances.[27] The provisions require that every person manufacturing, distributing, or dispensing any controlled substance or any person proposing to engage in the manufacture, distribution, or dispensation of any controlled substance obtain an annual registration pursuant to the rules and regulations promulgated by the Attorney General. The registration is obtained from the Attorney General.[28]

In determining whether an application for manufacture[29] or distribution[30] of controlled substances in Schedule I or II shall be approved and registration granted, the Attorney General considers the following factors:

(1) Maintenance of effective control against diversion of particular controlled substances into other than legitimate medical, scientific and industrial channels;

(2) Compliance with applicable state and local law;

(3) Prior conviction record of applicant under federal or state laws relating to the manufacture, distribution, or dispensing of such substances;

(4) Past experience in the distribution of controlled substances; and

(5) Such other factors as may be relevant to and consistent with the public health and safety.[31]

---

[26] For example, New Jersey and Louisiana classify the controlled substances into four schedules instead of five schedules. See, N.J. Rev. Stat. Sec. 24:21-1 et seq. (1971), La. Rev. Stat. Ann. Sec. 40:963 (1970).

[27] 21 U.S.C.A. 821-841 (1970).

[28] 21 U.S.C.A. 822 (1970).

[29] 21 U.S.C.A. 823(a) (1970).

[30] 21 U.S.C.A. 823(b) (1970).

[31] 21 U.S.C.A. 823(a), 823(b) (1970).

Registration to manufacture or distribute controlled substances in Schedules III, IV or V involve consideration of similar factors. One distinctive consideration, however, is the factor of whether the applicant has promoted technical advances in the art of manufacturing these substances and the development of new substances.[32]

The Attorney General is empowered to revoke or suspend any registration issued if it is established that the holder of the registration has falsified his application, lost his state license or been convicted of a felony violation relating to any controlled substance.[33] The Attorney General is authorized to limit revocation or suspension to the particular controlled substance to which grounds for revocation or suspension exist.[34]

The Attorney General is also empowered to set production quotas for the various controlled substances and set individual production quotas based on the estimated medical, scientific, research and industrial needs.[35]

All distribution of controlled substances in Schedule I or II must be made pursuant to a written order of the person to whom such substance is distributed and made on a form issued by the Attorney General.[36]

3. Offenses and Penalties[37]

A. UNLAWFUL MANUFACTURE OR DISTRIBUTION: Under federal law, it is unlawful to manufacture, distribute, or dispense or possess with intent to manufacture, distribute, or dispense a controlled substance or counterfeit substance. In the case of a controlled substance in Schedule I or II *which is a narcotic drug,*[38] committing the offense described above involves a sentence of

---

[32] 21 U.S.C.A. 823(d), 823(e) (1970).

[33] 21 U.S.C.A. 824 (1970).

[34] 21 U.S.C.A. 824(b) (1970).

[35] 21 U.S.C.A. 826(b) (1970).

[36] 21 U.S.C.A. 828 (1970).

[37] 21 U.S.C.A. 841-851 (1970).

[38] 21 U.S.C.A. 802 defines narcotic as: (A) opium, coca leaves and opiates, (B) A compound, manufacture salt, derivative, or preparation of opium, coca leaves, or opiates, (C) A substance (and any compound, manufacture salt derivative, or preparation thereof) which is chemically identical with any of the substances referred to in "A" or "B."

not more than 15 years imprisonment and a fine of not more than $25,000 or both for the first offense. Any subsequent offense involves a sentence of not more than 30 years imprisonment and a fine of not more than $50,000 or both. In the case of a controlled substance in Schedule I or II *which is not a narcotic drug,* or in the case of any controlled substance in Schedule III, the unlawful manufacture, dispensation, or distribution involves a sentence of not more than five years imprisonment or a fine of not more than $15,000 or both. A subsequent offense is punished by not more than ten years imprisonment, and a fine of not more than $30,000 or both.

If the offense involves a controlled substance in Schedule IV, the offender shall be sentenced to a term of imprisonment of not more than three years, a fine of not more than $10,000 or both. A subsequent offense involves a sentence of not more than six years imprisonment, a fine of not more than $20,000 or both.

If the offense involves a controlled substance in Schedule V, the offender can be sentenced to a term of imprisonment of not more than one year, a fine of not more than $5,000 or both. A subsequent offense involves a sentence of imprisonment of not more than two years, a fine of not more than $10,000 or both.[39]

It is, therefore, an offense punishable by law for any person to manufacture, distribute or sell any controlled substance or to create, distribute or possess with intent to distribute or dispense a counterfeit substance.[40]

Section 842 of 21 U.S.C.A. provides for the regulation of persons *who are registered* to manufacture, distribute, sell, or possess controlled substances. This section makes it unlawful for any person: (1) Who is subject to the requirements of Part C to distribute or dispense a controlled substance in Schedule II without the written prescription of a practitioner;[41] (2) Who is a registrant to distribute or dispense a controlled substance

---

[39] 21 U.S.C.A. 841(a)(1)(2), (b)(1)(A), (B), (2), (3) (1970). It is significant to note that 21 U.S.C.A. 841(b)4 specifically excludes marihuana from the penalties imposed by 21 U.S.C.A. 841 and provides for separate penalties pursuant to the provisions of 21 U.S.C.A. 844(a), (b) (1970).
[40] 21 U.S.C.A. 841(a)(1)(2) (1970).
[41] 21 U.S.C.A. 842(a)(1) (1970).

not authorized by his registration to another registrant or other authorized person or to manufacture a controlled substance not authorized by his registration;[42] (3) Who is a registrant to distribute a controlled substance which is not in a commercial container bearing an identification symbol;[43] (4) To remove, alter, or obliterate a symbol or label required by law;[44] (5) To refuse or fail to make, keep, or furnish any record, report, notification, declaration, order, or order form, statement, invoice, or information pursuant to the registration requirements;[45] (6) To refuse any entry into any premises or inspection of premises used to manufacture controlled substances;[46] (7) To remove, break, injure or deface a seal placed upon controlled substances or to remove or dispose of substances so placed under seal;[47] or (8) To use, to his own advantage, or to reveal other than to duly authorized officers or employees of the United States, or to the courts when relevant to any judicial proceeding under the *Drug Abuse Prevention and Control Act of 1970*, any information acquired in the course of an inspection authorized by this law concerning any method or process which as a trade secret is entitled to protection.[48]

The offenses described above regulate the registrants' manufacture of controlled substances and specific provisions aid in the establishment of controls to see that these provisions are complied with. For example, a registrant could deny the right to inspect the premises by contending that an inspection could result in a loss of vital trade secrets. This possibility is prevented by the provisional safeguard in 21 U.S.C.A. 842(a)(8) which provides that it is unlawful for any governmental agent to reveal these trade secrets to anyone other than other authorized officers or employees of the United States or in the courts when relevant to judicial proceedings where offenses of the federal drug laws are prosecuted.

---

[42] 21 U.S.C.A. 842(a)(2) (1970).
[43] 21 U.S.C.A. 842(a)(3) (1970).
[44] 21 U.S.C.A. 842(a)(4) (1970).
[45] 21 U.S.C.A. 842(a)(5) (1970).
[46] 21 U.S.C.A. 842(a)(b) (1970).
[47] 21 U.S.C.A. 842(a)(7) (1970).
[48] 21 U.S.C.A. 842(a)(8) (1970).

Section 842(b) makes it unlawful for any person who is a registrant to manufacture a controlled substance in Schedule I or II which is: (1) Not expressly authorized by his registration and by a quota assigned to him by the Attorney General; or (2) In excess of a quota assigned to him by the Attorney General.[49]

Violations of offenses described in Section 842(b) *Supra* involve the following penalties: (1) A civil penalty of not more than $25,000; (2) Or if prosecuted by any information or indictment alleging the violation was committed knowingly, imprisonment of not more than one year or a fine of not more than $25,000 or both. (3) A second or subsequent violation involves a sentence of not more than two years and/or a fine of $50,000 or both.[50]

It is significant to note that there is a distinction between the mere occurrence of a violation which is punished by a civil penalty of a $25,000 fine, and a violation which is knowingly committed which involves imprisonment of not more than one year, a $25,000 fine, or both.

Closely guarding the activities relating to the manufacture and distribution of controlled substances, the statute further provides that it is unlawful for any person knowingly or intentionally: (1) Who is a registrant to distribute a controlled substance classified in Schedule I or II, in the course of his legitimate business unless the distribution is pursuant to an order form issued by the Attorney General;[51] (2) To use in the course of the manufacture or distribution of a controlled substance a registration number which is fictitious, revoked, suspended, or issued to another person;[52] (3) To acquire or obtain possession of a controlled substance by misrepresentation, fraud, forgery, deception, or subterfuge;[53] (4) To furnish false or fraudulent material information in, or omit any material information from, any application, report, record, or other document required to be made, kept or filed by law;[54] or (5) To make, dis-

[49] 21 U.S.C.A. 842(b)(1)(2) (1970).
[50] 21 U.S.C.A. 842(c)(1)(2) (1970).
[51] 21 U.S.C.A. 843(a)(1) (1970).
[52] 21 U.S.C.A. 843(a)(2) (1970).
[53] 21 U.S.C.A. 843(a)(3) (1970).
[54] 21 U.S.C.A. 843(a)(4) (1970).

tribute or possess any punch, die, plate stone, or other thing designed to print, imprint, or reproduce the trademark, trade name, or other identifying mark, imprint, or device of another or any likeness of any of the foregoing upon any drug or container or labeling thereof so as to render such drug a counterfeit substance.[55]

It is also provided that it is unlawful to knowingly or intentionally use any communication facility in causing or facilitating the commission of any act or acts constituting a felony under any provision of the *Federal Drug Abuse Prevention and Control Act of 1970.*[56]

Any violation of the above described offenses is punishable by imprisonment of not more than four years, a fine of not more than $30,000 or both. A second or subsequent offense is punishable by imprisonment of not more than eight years, a fine of $60,000 or both.[57]

B. PENALTIES AND SIMPLE POSSESSION. It is unlawful for any person knowingly or intentionally, to possess a controlled substance unless it was obtained from a medical doctor directly or by his prescription. A violation of this provision is punishable by imprisonment of not more than one year, a fine of not more than $5,000 or both, in cases involving first offenders.[58] A second or subsequent offense is punishable by imprisonment of not more than two years, a fine of not more than $10,000, or both.[59]

The laws relating to offenses involving simple possession are comparatively less severe than those laws prevailing at state levels. Section 844 of 21 U.S.C.A. provides that if a person has never been found guilty of any law of the United States relating to narcotic drugs, marihuana or depressant or stimulant substances he may be conditionally discharged. In these instances involving first offenders found quilty of unlawful possession of a controlled substance, the court may, without entering a judgment of guilty, and with the consent of such persons, defer

---

[55] 21 U.S.C.A. 843(a)(5) (1970).
[56] 21 U.S.C.A. 843(b) (1970).
[57] 21 U.S.C.A. 843(c) (1970).
[58] 21 U.S.C.A. 844(a) (1970).
[59] *Ibid.*

further proceedings and place the person on probation upon such reasonable conditions as may require and for a period not to exceed one year. If the person complies with the probationary terms the court has the power to dismiss the charges against him at the end of his term of probation. The discharge and dismissal are not considered a conviction of a crime.[60]

The concept of permitting the first offender the opportunity of rehabilitation is extended to greater limits in instances involving persons not over 21 years of age. One of the most significant provisions of the federal law states that if the person is not over 21 years of age at the time of being found guilty of simple possession of any controlled substance and if the first offender is dismissed and discharged from criminal proceedings upon satisfactory compliance with the probationary terms, such person may apply to the court to expunge all records of the criminal proceedings. The effect of such an expungement order is to restore such person in the contemplation of the law, to the status he occupied before such arrest, indictment or probation.[61] It is significant to note that many of the states which adopt the federal dangerous drug law by adopting and enacting the Uniform Controlled Substances Law do not include the provisions relating to conditional discharge and expungement of criminal records.[62] It is, therefore, evident that many of the states which adopt the federal controlled substance classifications are not willing to accept the federal legislative intent in entirety.

c. Comparing Simple Possession Offenses to Offenses Involving Unlawful Manufacture or Distribution of Controlled Substances. (1) Simple possession of controlled sub-

---

[60] 21 U.S.C.A. 844(b)(1) (1970).

[61] 21 U.S.C.A. 844(b)(2) (1970). The federal legislative philosophy of permitting the first offender having criminal proceedings dismissed and discharged, and in the case of those under 21 years of age, having all criminal records expunged, can be contrasted to the legislative intent at state levels for purposes of illustrating the polarized attitudes which prevail when considering penalties to be imposed for possession of dangerous drugs. The Texas Penal Code, Section 725(b) (Supp. 1969-70) imposes a punishment of two years to life for first offenses involving possession of marihuana. There are no statutory provisions for conditional discharge of criminal proceedings or expungement of criminal records for offenders not over 21 years of age.

[62] See generally, Va. Code Ann. Sec. 54-524-1 et seq. (Supp. 1970).

Table II—Federal Law Aim
Drug Abuse Prevention and Control

Type of Drug	Manufacture or Possession With Intent to Manufacture or Distribution or Possession With Intent to Distribute	Manufacture Not Expres: Authorized by Registrati or Manufacture in Excess Assigned Quota
Schedule I 42 Opiates 22 Opium Derivatives 17 Hallucinogenic substances	Narcotic: 1st: NMT 15 yrs. and/or $25,000 S: NMT 30 yrs. and/or NMT $50,000 Non-narcotic: 1st: NMT 5 yrs. and/or $15,000 S: NMT 10 yrs. and/or $30,000	1st: Civil Penalty, $25,00 committed knowingly, 1 y and/or $25,000 S: NMT 2 yrs. and/or $50
Schedule II Opium, opiate, opium poppy, poppy straw, coca leaves, 21 specific opiates, and any injectable liquid containing methamphetamine	1st: NMT 5 yrs. and/or $15,000 S: NMT 10 yrs. and/or $30,000	1st: Civil Penalty, $25,00 committed knowingly, 1 y and/or $25,000 S: NMT 2 yrs. and/or $50
Schedule III Amphetamine, phenmetrazine, methamphetamine (except injectable liquid) methylphenidate, 10 specific substances having a depressant effect upon the central nervous system, nalorphine, compounds containing limited quantities of narcotic drugs	1st: NMT 5 yrs. and/or $15,000 S: NMT 10 yrs. and/or $30,000	1st: Civil Penalty, $25,00 committed knowingly, 1 y and/or $25,000 S: NMT 2 yrs. and/or $50
Schedule IV Barbital, chloral betaine, chloral hydrate, ethcloruynol, ethinamate, methohexital, meprobamate, methylphenobarbital, paraldehyde, petrichloral, phenobarbital	1st: NMT 3 yrs. and/or $10,000 S: NMT 6 yrs. and/or $20,000	1st: Civil Penalty, $25,00 committed knowingly, 1 y and/or $25,000 S: NMT 2 yrs. and/or $50
Schedule V Specific compounds having valuable medicinal qualities containing limited quantities of narcotic drugs	1st: NMT 1 yr. and/or $5,000 S: NMT 2 yrs. and/or $10,000	1st: Civil Penalty, $25,00 committed knowingly, 1 y and/or $25,000 S: NMT 2 yrs. and/or $50

Controlling Drug Abuse

1970—21 U.S.C. 801 et seq. (1970)

*Distributing a Controlled Substance Without Proper Use of an Order Form; Using a Fictitious Registration Number**	*Simple Possession*	*Distribution to a Minor*	*Person Engaged in Continuing Criminal Enterprise*
t: NMT 4 yrs. and/or NMT $30,000 NMT 8 yrs. and/or NMT $60,000	1st: NMT 1 yr. and/or NMT $5,000 S: NMT 2 yrs. and/or NMT $5,000	1st: Twice penalty authorized for distribution to adults S: 3 times penalty authorized for distribution to adults	1st: 10 yrs. to life and NMT $100,000 S: 20 yrs. to life and NMT $200,000
t: NMT 4 yrs. and/or NMT $30,000 NMT 8 yrs. and/or NMT $60,000	1st: NMT 1 yr. and/or NMT $5,000 S: NMT 2 yrs. and/or NMT $5,000	1st: Twice penalty authorized for distribution to adults S: 3 times penalty authorized for distribution to adults	1st: 10 yrs. to life and NMT $100,000 S: 20 yrs. to life and NMT $200,000
t: NMT 4 yrs. and/or NMT $30,000 NMT 8 yrs. and/or NMT $60,000	1st: NMT 1 yr. and/or NMT $5,000 S: NMT 2 yrs. and/or NMT $5,000	1st: Twice penalty authorized for distribution to adults S: 3 times penalty authorized for distribution to adults	1st: 10 yrs. to life and NMT $100,000 S: 20 yrs. to life and NMT $200,000
t: NMT 4 yrs. and/or NMT $30,000 NMT 8 yrs. and/or NMT $60,000	1st: NMT 1 yr. and/or NMT $5,000 S: NMT 2 yrs. and/or NMT $5,000	1st: Twice penalty authorized for distribution to adults S: 3 times penalty authorized for distribution to adults	1st: 10 yrs. to life and NMT $100,000 S: 20 yrs. to life and NMT $200,000
t: NMT 4 yrs. and/or NMT $30,000 NMT 8 yrs. and/or NMT $60,000	1st: NMT 1 yr. and/or NMT $5,000 S: NMT 2 yrs. and/or NMT $5,000	1st: Twice penalty authorized for distribution to adults S: 3 times penalty authorized for distribution to adults	1st: 10 yrs. to life and NMT $100,000 S: 20 yrs. to life and NMT $200,000

* Possession or distribution of anything used to create counterfeit drugs, labels or containers; e intentional use of any communication facility while violating any provisions of the act.

stances is punished without considering which schedule the unlawfully possessed drug is classified under. In contrast, penalties imposed for the unlawful manufacture, or distribution of a controlled substance pivot on a primary consideration of which schedule the controlled substance is classified under. If the substance falls within Schedule I or II an ancillary consideration is whether or not the controlled substance is a narcotic.

(2) Severe criminal penalties are imposed for offenses involving manufacture and distribution. Sentences imposed for offenses involving simple possession are less severe, and liberal provisions encourage the court to conditionally discharge criminal proceedings against first offenders and expunge criminal records of youthful first offenders.

D. DISTRIBUTION OF CONTROLLED SUBSTANCES TO PERSONS UNDER 21. Very harsh criminal penalties are provided in instances where a person over 18 years of age distributes a controlled substance to a person under 21. The federal law imposes twice the amount of punishment for these offenses than for distribution to persons over 21 years of age. For example, a first offender selling or distributing a controlled substance to a minor would be punishable by not more than 30 years imprisonment and a fine of not more than $50,000, or both, if a Schedule I or II narcotic drug is involved.[63] A second or subsequent violation of the law prohibiting distribution of controlled substances to minors is punishable by three times the penalty imposed for ordinary distribution.[64] Therefore, in a case of a second or subsequent offense, a sentence could involve up to 45 years imprisonment, a $75,000 fine, or both, for a narcotic Schedule I or II substance.

E. CONTINUING CRIMINAL ENTERPRISE. In an effort to repel the forces of organized crime, the federal law provides that any person who engages in a continuing criminal enterprise and violates the federal drug laws, *shall* be sentenced to a term of imprisonment which may *not be less than ten years* and which may be up to life imprisonment, a fine of not more than $100,000 and a forfeiture of income derived from such enterprise. A second or

---

[63] 21 U.S.C.A. 845(a) (1970).
[64] 21 U.S.C.A. 845(b) (1970).

subsequent offense involves a sentence of *not less than* 20 years and which may be up to life imprisonment, a fine of not more than $200,000, and forfeiture of income derived from the continuing criminal enterprise.[65] The statute indicates a person is engaged in a continuing criminal enterprise if: (1) he violates a provision of the federal dangerous drug laws, the punishment for which is a felony, and (2) such violation is a part of a continuing series of violations of the *Federal Drug Abuse Prevention and Control Act of 1970*:[66] (a) which are undertaken by such person in concert with five or more persons with respect to whom such person occupies a position of organizer, a supervisory position, or any other position of management, and, (b) from which such person obtains substantial income or resources.[67]

It is most significant that the sentences imposed are mandatory, the only offense which involves a mandatory sentence is being a member of a continuing criminal enterprise and there can be no suspended or probated sentence.[68] There have been some strong arguments indicating that the language in the statute is vague and does not clearly define the offense. For example, it has been suggested that it is not clear what constitutes a "continuing series of violations," and what is meant by deriving "substantial income or resources" from the enterprise.[69]

---

[65] 21 U.S.C.A. 848 (1970).
[66] *Op. cit., Supra,* Note 1.
[67] 21 U.S.C.A. 848(b) (1970).
[68] 21 U.S.C.A. 848(c) (1970).
[69] See, 1970 U.S. Code Cong. and Adm. News, p-5711.

CHAPTER IV

STATE DRUG ABUSE LAWS

Alabama: Ala. Code Tit. 22, Sec. 225-258 (Supp. 1970)

THE 1969 AMENDMENTS to the laws of Alabama include legislative attempts to curb the abuse of the opiates and the narcotics which are derived from opium such as morphine and heroin. The amendments also include prohibitions involving amphetamines, barbiturates and hallucinogenic drugs. In addition to the chapter relating to narcotics and poisonous drugs, the Alabama legislature enacted the *Alabama Drug Abuse Control Act.* This chapter prohibits the manufacture (except by those permitted and registered to do so), sale, delivery, or possession of depressant or stimulant drugs. It also provides guidelines for those lawfully manufacturing or possessing stimulant and depressant drugs which require that complete and accurate records be kept relating to the proper dispensation of drugs.

1. MARIHUANA: A separate chapter of the act has responded to the need of prohibiting the unlawful possession, transportation, delivery, sale, offering for sale or giving away in any form any marihuana or any derivative of marihuana. In addition the law now prohibits the sale, delivery, possession or giving away of any synthetic equivalent of the substances contained in the plant. The prohibitions relating to the synthetic equivalents illustrate that chemical equivalents were being used for purposes of avoiding the prohibitions set forth in earlier laws. The prohibitions relating to possession of marihuana or any of its derivatives are quite harsh. A first offender may receive not less than two nor more than ten years and in addition may be fined not more than $20,000. A second offender will receive not less than five nor more than ten years and may be fined not more than $20,000. For any subsequent offense the offender will receive not less than ten nor more than 40 years, and in addition, may be fined not more than $20,000. It is significant to note that there can be no suspended sentence or probation if the conviction is

TABLE III—ALABAMA

Citation	Type of Drug	General Penalty Provisions	Possession	Possession With Intent to sell	Sale and Similar Transactions	Sale to Minor by Adult
Ala. Code Tit. 22, Sec. 225-258 (Supp. 1970).	Narcotic: Heroin, Hallucinogen and other psychotomimetics (not including marihuana)		1st: 5-20 and NMT $20,000 S: 10-40 and NMT $20,000	1st: 5-20 and NMT $20,000 S: 10-40 and NMT $20,000	1st: 5-20 and NMT $20,000 S: 10-40 and NMT $20,000	10 yrs. to life or death if jury directs; NMT $20,000
	Amphetamines and Barbiturates	1st: NMT 1 yr. and/or $500 2nd: NMT 2 yrs. and/or $1,000				
	Marihuana		1st: 2-10 yrs. and/or NMT $20,000 2nd: 5-20 yrs. and/or NMT $20,000 S: 10-40 yrs. and/or NMT $20,000		1st: 5-20 yrs. and/or NMT $20,000 S: 10-40 yrs. and/or NMT $20,000	1st 10-40 yrs. and/or NMT $20,000

1st = 1st offense.
2nd = 2nd offense.
3rd = 3rd offense.
S = Subsequent offense.

NMT = Not more than.
NLT = Not less than.

the offender's second or subsequent offense. The penalties for first offenses involving possession of marihuana are much more harsh than in many other states.

The penalties imposed for delivering, selling, offering to sell, bartering, furnishing, or giving away of marihuana, its derivatives and those synthetic substances containing similar chemical structures are greater than those penalties imposed upon those merely possessing marihuana. In these instances a first offender is guilty of a felony and upon conviction for a first offense the accused will be imprisoned in the penitentiary for not less than five nor more than 20 years and, in addition, may be fined not more than $20,000; and upon conviction for a second or subsequent offense the penalty is not less than ten nor more than 40 years and a possible fine of not more than $20,000.

If the sale, delivery or giving away is made by a person over 18 years of age to a person under 18 years of age then the offender shall upon conviction be imprisoned not less than ten years nor more than 40 years, and in addition may be fined not more than $20,000. In such cases there is no suspension of sentence and probation is not granted.

The Alabama laws relating to the violations involving heroin and other narcotic drugs carry stronger penalties than those involving marihuana. The law treats possession of heroin as harshly as it does the sale of heroin. The first offense carries a minimum sentence of five years in contrast to the minimum of two years for the possession of marihuana. The maximum sentence for the first offender is 20 years as contrasted to the ten year maximum for a similar offense involving marihuana.

If an adult sells heroin to a minor, whether it is a first offense or a subsequent offense the sentence ranges from ten years to life and not more than a $20,000 fine. Alternatively, the jury may in its discretion impose the death penalty.

2. BARBITURATES AND AMPHETAMINES: Barbiturates are carefully regulated by laws which require that all substances containing the salts and derivatives of barbituric acid be handled, sold and distributed pursuant to the provisions requiring a prescription before the drugs are used. A violation of any of these pro-

visions brings a maximum penalty of one year and is treated as a misdemeanor with a possible fine of $500 for the first offense.

In the 1969 amendments the legislature enacted a chapter entitled, "Amphetamines and other Stimulating Drugs." The legislature stated that it was the purpose of the chapter to control the possession, dispensing, handling, sale and distribution of amphetamines and/or other stimulating drugs. Only a pharmacist may deliver the drug if there is an original written prescription by a doctor. It is also a misdemeanor for a person to possess this type of drug without having obtained it by prescription. The penalties for violating these provisions are similar to those involving the barbiturates. The first offender may be imprisoned for one year and/or receive a fine of not more than $500. The second offender may be imprisoned for not more than two years and/or receive a fine of not more than $1,000.

3. HALLUCINOGENIC DRUGS: (LSD-25, Psilocybin and other Psychotomimetics). A separate chapter of the Alabama laws makes it unlawful to possess, transport, deliver, sell or give away in any form lysergic acid diethylamide (LSD-25), psilocybin, or any similar drug or substance which is classified as a psychotomimetic drug or substance which produces an hallucinatory effect or induces a schizophrenic psychosis.

The same penalty attaches for illegal possession of these substances as for the illegal sale of this type of drug. The first offender is imprisoned for not less than five years nor more than 20 years and in addition may be fined not more than $20,000. For a second or subsequent offense the minimum sentence is ten years with a maximum sentence of 40 years. The penalties are similar to those for offenses involving heroin.

The statute relating to the hallucinogenic drugs does not apply to physicians, dentists, drug manufacturers, hospitals, drug wholesalers, apothecaries and certain laboratories. These are exempted because of the purported therapeutic use of these drugs.

It is interesting to note that in offenses involving heroin or any of the hallucinogenic drugs, illegal possession is treated statutorily as harshly as the illegal sale of these substances. This is in contrast to the penalties imposed in marihuana offenses where the possession of marihuana is not treated as harshly as the sale of marihuana.

There is a significant contrast in penalties invoked for offenses involving amphetamines and barbiturates and offenses involving narcotics, hallucinogens and marihuana.

Alaska: Alaska Stat. Sec. 17.10.010-.240 (Supp. 1970)

The laws of Alaska are adopted from the *Uniform Narcotic Drug Act.* Marihuana is not classified as a narcotic drug in Alaska but is put in the category of depressant, hallucinogenic and stimulant drugs for purposes of imposing penalties for manufacture, sale or possession.

Possession and sale of narcotic drugs are punished similarly by statute unless the sale is made by an adult to a minor. The first offense for possession or sale of a narcotic drug involves a two to ten year sentence and not more than a $5,000 fine. A second offense brings a ten to 20 year sentence and a fine of not more than $7,500. Any subsequent offense carries a 20 to 40 year sentence and a fine of not more than $25,000. Any subsequent violation of the law prohibiting the sale of a narcotic drug by an adult to a minor carries a life sentence. A person who provides information which leads to the arrest and conviction of another on the charge of unlawfully selling narcotic drugs to a minor is eligible for a reward of $1,000.

1. Drugs (specifically enumerated substances requiring prescription): It is unlawful for a person to sell, give away, barter, exchange or distribute more than one grain or fluid ounce of barbital, amytal, luminal or veronal without doing so by order of prescription of a physician, dentist, surgeon or veterinary surgeon licensed to practice in the State of Alaska. The penalty for the unlawful sale of these substances is punishable by a fine of not less than $100 nor more than $500 and/or imprisonment for not more than 180 days.

2. Depressant, Hallucinogenic and Stimulant Drugs: In defining the drugs which come within the purview of this provision, the statute includes cannabis (all parts of the plant *cannabis sativa;* marihuana), barbiturates, amphetamines, the hallucinogenics such as psilocybin, diemethyltryptamine, LSD, and

TABLE IV—ALASKA

Citation	Type of Drug	General Penalty Provisions	Possession	Possession for Sale	Sale	Sale to Minor by Adult
Alaska Stat. Sec. 17.10.010.240 (Supp. 1970).	Narcotic (not including Marihuana).	1st: 2-10 yrs. and NMT $5,000 2nd: 10-20 yrs. and NMT $7,500 S: 20-40 yrs. and NMT $10,000				1st: 10-30 yrs. and $5,000-$10,000 2nd: 15-30 yrs. and NMT $25,000
	Stimulant, Depressant, Hallucinogenic (including Marihuana).		NMT 1 year and/or $1,000		1st: 1-25 yrs. and/ or $20,000 S: Maximum life and/or $25,000	S: life maximum and/or $25,000 Maximum life and/or $25,000

1st = 1st offense.
2nd = 2nd offense.

3rd = 3rd offense.
S = Subsequent offense.

NMT = Not more than.
NLT = Not less than.

any other drug which is found to contain any quantity of a substance which has a potential for abuse because of its depressant or stimulant effect on the central nervous system or any drug which has a potential for abuse because of its hallucinogenic effect.

The unlawful possession of marihuana, amphetamines, barbiturates or hallucinogens described within this provision are treated as a misdemeanor and is punishable by imprisonment for not more than one year and/or by a fine of not more than $1,000.

Any other offense such as possession for sale, disposal or distribution of the drugs classified as stimulant, depressant or hallucinogenic drugs carry harsher sentences. A first offense carries a sentence of not more than 25 years and/or a fine of not more than $20,000. Any subsequent offense involves a sentence of any term of years or life imprisonment and/or a fine of $25,000.

If a person sells or disposes of a depressant, hallucinogenic or stimulant drug to a person less than 19 years of age, he is guilty of a felony and upon conviction is punishable by imprisonment for any term of years to life or by a fine of $25,000, or by both.

It is interesting to note that Alaska has grouped marihuana, amphetamines, barbiturates and the hallucinogenic drugs together for purposes of preventing drug abuse. This is a realistic grouping since many barbiturates, when abused, induce hallucinations, and marihuana is now classified as an hallucinogen under the *Federal Drug Abuse Prevention and Control Act of 1970*.

Arizona: Ariz. Rev. Stat. Ann., Sec. 36-1001 to 1002.10-1017
(Supp. 1969), Ariz. Rev. Stat. Ann., Sec. 32-1901
(Supp. 1969)

The *Uniform Narcotic Drug Act* of Arizona contains severe restrictions relating to narcotics and marihuana. The laws of this state do not equally punish offenders abusing other drugs such as amphetamines, barbiturates or hallucinogens.

The laws relating to narcotics and marihuana do provide some interesting variations from the laws of other states. In an effort to prevent the importation and transportation of narcotic drugs and marihuana into the state, Arizona has enacted specific pro-

TABLE V—ARIZONA

Citation	Type of Drug	Possession	Possession for Sale	Sale	Sale to Minor by Adult
Ariz. Rev. Stat. Ann., Sec. 36-1001 to 1002.10-1017 (Supp. 1969).	Narcotic	1st: 2-10 yrs. 2nd: 5-20 yrs. S: 15 yrs. to life	1st: 5-15 yrs. 2nd: NLT 10 yrs. S: NLT 15 yrs.	1st: 5-15 yrs. 2nd: NLT 10 yrs. S: NLT 15 yrs.	1st: 10 yrs. to life but NLT 5 yrs. in prison 2nd: 10 yrs. to life but NLT 10 yrs. in prison S: 15 yrs. to life but NLT 15 yrs. in prison
	Marihuana	1st: 1-10 yrs. or 1 yr. in county jail and/or $1,000 fine. 2nd: 2-20 yrs. S: 5 yrs. to life	1st: 2-10 yrs. 2nd: 5-15 yrs. S: 10 yrs. to life	1st: 5 yrs.-life 2nd: 5 yrs.-life S: 10 yrs.-life	1st: 10 yrs.-life 2nd: 10 yrs.-life S: 15 yrs.-life
Ariz. Rev. Stat. Ann., Sec. 32-1901 (Supp. 1969).	Dangerous Drugs, Hallucinogens, Barbiturates and Amphetamines (including LSD)	1st and S: 1-10 yrs. and/or $5,000 or 1 yr. in county jail and/or $1,000	1st and S: 1 yr. to life	1st and S: 1 yr. to life	1st and S: 1 yr. to life

1st = 1st offense.
2nd = 2nd offense.

3rd = 3rd offense.
S = Subsequent offense.

NMT = Not more than.
NLT = Not less than.

hibitions against such importation and transportation. The penalties involved are very severe and these penalties exist distinct from the traditional penalties which are imposed for possession, sale or sale to a minor. The purpose of these separate provisions is to limit the flow of these drugs into the state.

Although marihuana is defined as a narcotic drug in the section of the chapter defining narcotics, the legislature enacted separate provisions relating to prohibitions involving marihuana. Therefore, the following provisions are applicable to cases involving opium and any of the derivatives such as morphine, codeine and heroin. The prohibitions are also directed at cocaine and any derivative of coca leaves which contains cocaine.

Possession of a narcotic drug carries a sentence of two to ten years for the first offense and one to 20 years for a second offense. Any subsequent offense carries a penalty of 15 years to life. A *sale* of a narcotic drug will lead to a five to 15 year sentence for a first offense and a sentence of not less than ten years for a second offense. Any subsequent offense carries a minimum sentence of 15 years.

A *sale* of a narcotic to a *minor* by an adult requires that the convicted person receive a sentence of ten years to life with not less than five years of the sentence served in prison. A second offense also entails a sentence of ten years to life but a minimum of ten years must be served as a prison sentence. Any subsequent offense involves a sentence of 15 years to life and not less than 15 years must be served in prison.

Inducing a minor to violate the narcotics law carries a sentence of ten years to life for a first offender, ten years to life for a second offender, and 15 years to life for any subsequent offense.

Importing or transporting a narcotic drug into Arizona involves a five year to life sentence for a first offense, or ten years to life sentence for a second offense and 15 years to life for any subsequent offense. This section, directed at preventing the narcotic drugs from entering the state, is quite unique.

As mentioned above, although marihuana is defined as a narcotic drug, the penalties for varied offenses involving marihuana are set forth separately in the *Uniform Narcotic Drug Act of Arizona.*

Possession of marihuana is punishable by a sentence of one to ten years for a first offense, one to 20 years for a second offense and 15 years to life for any subsequent offense. This is in contrast to some of the lesser penalties involved in other states. *Possessing* marihuana for the purpose of making a sale is punishable by a sentence of two to ten years for a first offense, five to 15 years for a second offense and ten years to life for any subsequent offense.

A sale of marihuana and any similar transaction carries a penalty of five years to life for the first offense, five years to life for the second offense and ten years to life for any subsequent offense.

The importation and transportation of marihuana into the state of Arizona is discouraged by imposing a sentence of five years to life upon a first offender whereby a minimum of three years must be served. The second offender will receive a sentence of five years to life also but a minimum of five years must be served. Any subsequent offense carries a sentence of ten years to life with a minimum of ten years which must be served in prison.

The act tries to deter adults from inducing minors to use marihuana by punishing such an offense with a sentence of ten years to life for the first offense, ten years to life for the second offense (with the time served before eligibility for probation being different) and 15 years to life for any subsequent offense.

The distinguishing characteristics of the *Uniform Narcotic Drug Act of Arizona* are the provisions which specifically attempt to prevent importation and transportation of narcotics into the state. In addition, the provisions not only provide penalties for an adult who induces a minor to violate the narcotic drug laws but also provide penalties for minors inducing other minors to violate the narcotic drug laws. This is similar to the provisions set forth in California.

A separate statute provides penalties for offenses involving hallucinogens (LSD), amphetamines and barbiturates. These penalties are not as harsh as the penalties imposed for violations involving those substances defined as narcotic drugs.

Arkansas: Ark. Stat. Ann. Sec. 82-1001 et seq. (Supp. 1969), Ark. Stat. Ann Sec. 82-2101 et seq. (Supp. 1969), Ark. Stat. Ann. Sec. 82-2110 et seq. (Supp. 1969)

The *Uniform Narcotic Drug Act* of Arkansas takes a broad approach in defining "narcotic" drugs. The act states that "narcotic drugs" means coca leaves, opium cannabis (marihuana) and every other substance neither chemically nor physically distinguishable from them. The act also gives the State Health Officer the power to include all drugs which he finds are narcotic in character and dangerous to the public health or have a potential for abuse because they have addiction-forming or addiction-sustaining results upon the user. The provision is based upon the power to prevent the abuse of those substances which threaten harm to the public health, safety, or morals.

The State Health Officer is to use the federal narcotic laws as guidelines in formulating the definitions of narcotic drugs. It is reasonable to assume that under the *Federal Comprehensive Drug Abuse Prevention and Control Act of 1970* this will present some difficulties because of the five types of schedules which have been created by the federal government in an attempt to classify substances which have a potential for abuse. Since the drug laws of Arkansas merely set forth general penalty provisions for the sale, manufacture, distribution or possession of *all* narcotic drugs, it is difficult to ascertain how the State Health Officer would be able to classify a regulated substance by using the federal narcotic laws as a guideline.

It is significant to note that in Arkansas there are special provisions made within the statute for the abuse of such drugs as amphetamines, barbiturates or the hallucinogens.

The sentence imposed for the illegal manufacture, sale, possession or distribution of a narcotic drug is two to five years and a fine of not more than $2,000 for the first offense. The second offender may receive a sentence of five to ten years and a fine of not more than $2,000. A third offense is punishable by imprisonment of ten to 20 years and a fine of not more than $2,000.

TABLE VI—ARKANSAS

Citation	Type of Drug	General Penalty Provisions
Ark. Stat. Ann., Sec. 82-1001 et seq. (Supp. 1969).	Narcotic	1st: 2-5 yrs. and NMT $2,000 2nd: 5-10 yrs. and $2,000 3rd: 10-20 yrs. and $2,000
Ark. Stat. Ann., Sec. 82-2101 et seq. (Supp. 1969).	Dangerous Drugs: Amphetamines, Barbiturates	1st: $2,000 and/or NMT 2 yrs. 2nd: 3-5 yrs. and/or $2,000 S: 5-10 yrs. and/or $5,000
Ark. Stat. Ann., Sec. 82-2110 et seq. (Supp. 1969).	Hallucinogens, LSD, DMT	1st: 3-5 yrs. S: 5-10 yrs.

1st = 1st offense.
2nd = 2nd offense.

3rd = 3rd offense.
S = Subsequent offense.

NMT = Not more than.
NLT = Not less than.

It is apparent that Arkansas has not chosen, as some other states have, to engage in the sophisticated classification of drugs for purposes of imposing varied penalties. The nature of the offense (possession, sale, or manufacture) and the type of drug, play no role in determining the penalty to be imposed. The State Health Officer undoubtedly executes a great degree of discretion in determining which drugs are to be defined as "narcotic drugs."

Separate provisions of the Arkansas statute are directed at abuse of drugs such as amphetamines, barbiturates and hallucinogens. The general penalty provisions for offenses involving hallucinogens are almost as harsh as the provisions directed at offenses involving narcotic drugs. The general penalty provisions for offenses involving amphetamines and barbiturates are also as harsh as the penalties imposed by offenses involving narcotics and hallucinogens.

California: Cal. Health and S. Code, Sec. 11500 et seq. (Supp. 1970)

California has adopted the policy of classifying marihuana separately from the other narcotic drugs for purposes of imposing penalties for the possession, sale or transportation of this substance into the state. The penalties imposed for offenses involving marihuana are less severe than the penalties imposed for violations involving other drugs.

Offenses which are treated separately are possession, addiction, possession for sale, sale, sales by a minor to an adult, inducing minors to violate the drug laws and forging prescriptions. Each of these separate offenses involves a different punishment. In addition, the punishment will differ depending on the type of drug involved. The California legislation reflects the necessity of each state developing drug laws which respond to specific drug problems within that state. In California the use of peyote was quite prevalent and the effort to curb this abuse is reflected in the provision of the drug laws which is specifically directed at the use of peyote. This provision states that every person who plants, cultivates, harvests, dries or possesses any plant of the genus Lophophora (peyote) shall be imprisoned in the county jail for not more than one year or the state prison for a period of not

TABLE VII—CALIFORNIA

Citation	Type of Drug	Possession	Possession for Sale	Sale and Similar Transactions	Sale to Minor by Adult
Cal. Health and S. Code, Sec. 11500 et seq. (Supp. 1970).	Narcotics	1st: 2-10 yrs. 2nd: 5-20 yrs. S:15 yrs. to life		1st: 5-15 yrs. 2nd: NLT 10 yrs. S: NLT 15 yrs.	1st: 10 yrs. to life mandatory 5 yrs. in prison 2nd: 10 yrs. to life mandatory 10 yrs. in prison S: 15 yrs. to life mandatory 5 yrs. in prison
	Marihuana	1st: county jail for NMT 1 yr. or state prison 1-10 yrs. 2nd: 2-20 yrs. S: 5 yrs. to life	1st: 2-10 yrs. 2nd: 5-15 yrs. S: 10 yrs.-life	1st: 5 yrs. to life 2nd: 5 yrs. to life S: 10 yrs. to life	1st: 5 yrs. to life 2nd: 10 yrs. to life S: 10 yrs. to life
	Other Dangerous Drugs: Ampheta- mines, Barbitu- burates, Hallucinogens	1st: county jail for NMT 1 yr. and/or state prison for 1-10 yrs. 2nd: 2-20 yrs.	1st: 2-10 yrs. 2nd: 5-15 yrs. S: 10 yrs. to life	1st: 5 yrs. to life 2nd: 5 yrs. to life S: 10 yrs. to life	1st: 10 yrs. to life 2nd: 10 yrs. to life S: 15 yrs. to life

1st = 1st offense.
2nd = 2nd offense.

3rd = 3rd offense.
S = Subsequent offense.

NMT = Not more than.
NLT = Not less than.

more than ten years. If such person has been previously convicted of any offense involving drugs then the sentence carries a minimum of two years and a maximum of 20 years.

The statutes imposing penalties for the varied offenses are directed at three main categories: (1) narcotics, (2) marihuana, (3) hallucinogens, amphetamines and barbiturates.

Marihuana is not defined as a narcotic and a first offense involving possession of the drug is punished as a misdemeanor.

Colorado: Colo. Rev. Stat. Ann. Sec. 48-5-1 et seq. (1963),
Colo. Rev. Stat. Ann. Sec. 48-8-1 et seq. (1963)

The Colorado drug laws prescribe similar punishment for offenses involving marihuana and other narcotic drugs. However, peyote is treated separately. The use, possession for sale, giving away, or any exchange of peyote is treated as a misdemeanor and carries a fine of not less than $100 nor more than $300 and/or imprisonment of 60 days to one year for first offenders. In cases involving second offenders, the violation is treated as a felony and is punishable by imprisonment of one to three years.

The State Board of Health has the power to classify and define a drug as addiction-forming or addiction-sustaining if notice and opportunity are provided for a hearing. Marihuana is not distinguished from the narcotic substances.

Separate statutes are aimed at preventing offenses which involve hallucinogens, amphetamines and barbiturates. The punishments imposed for offenses involving these drugs are significantly less than the penalties imposed for offenses involving narcotic drugs.

Connecticut: Conn. Gen. Stat. Ann. Sec. 19-443 et seq.
(Supp. 1969)

The provisions of the Connecticut laws reflect legislative attempts to control drug abuse at *all* levels. The legislature has defined the "abuse of drugs" as meaning, "the use of controlled drugs solely for their stimulant, depressant or hallucinogenic effect upon the higher functions of the central nervous system and not as a therapeutic agent prescribed in the course of med-

TABLE VIII—COLORADO

Citation	Type of Drug	Possession	Sale	Possession for Sale	Sale to Minor by Adult
Colo. Rev. Stat. Ann., Sec. 48-5-1 et seq. (1963).	Narcotics (including Marihuana)	1st: 2-15 yrs. and $10,000 2nd: NMT $10,000 and 5-20 yrs. S: NMT $10,000 and 10-30 yrs.	1st: 10-20 yrs. 2nd: 15-30 yrs. S: 20-40 yrs.	1st: 10-20 yrs. 2nd: 15-30 yrs. S: 20-40 yrs.	
Colo. Rev. Stat. Ann., Sec. 48-8-1 et seq. (1963).	Amphetamines, Barbiturates, Hallucinogens	1st: NMT 1 yr. and/or $500 2nd: NMT 2 yrs. and/or NMT $1,000 S: 1-14 yrs. and/or NMT $2,000	1st: 1-14 yrs. and/or NMT $1,000 2nd: 5-30 yrs. and/or NMT $5,000	1st: 1-14 yrs. and/or NMT $1,000 2nd: 5-30 yrs. and/or NMT $5,000	1st: 1-14 yrs. and/or NMT $1,000 2nd: 5-30 yrs. and/or NMT $5,000

1st = 1st offense.
2nd = 2nd offense.
3rd = 3rd offense.
S = Subsequent offense.

NMT = Not more than.
NLT = Not less than.

TABLE IX—CONNECTICUT

Citation	Type of Drug	Possession	Possession for Sale	Sale and Similar Transactions
Conn. Gen. Stat. Ann., Sec. 19-443 et seq. (Supp. 1969)	Narcotics	1st: NMT 5 yrs. and/or NMT $3,000 2nd: NMT 15 yrs. or NMT $5,000 or both S: NMT 25 yrs. and/or $10,000	1st: 5-10 yrs. and NMT $3,000 2nd: 10-15 yrs. and NMT $5,000 S: 25 yrs.	1st: 5-10 yrs. and NMT $3,000 2nd: 10-15 yrs. and NMT $5,000 S: 25 yrs.
	Hallucinogens, Amphetamines, Barbiturates	NMT 1 yr. and/or NMT $1,000		1st: NMT 2 yrs. and/or NMT $1,000 2nd: NMT 10 yrs. and/or $5,000

1st = 1st offense.   3rd = 3rd offense.   NMT = Not more than.
2nd = 2nd offense.   S = Subsequent offense.   NLT = Not less than.

ical treatment or in a program of research operated under the direction of a physician or pharmacologist."

The drugs which are considered "controlled drugs" are classified as cannabis-type drugs, cocaine-type drugs, amphetamine-type drugs, barbiturate-type drugs, morphine-type drugs and hallucinogenic-type drugs.

The possession of controlled drugs in Connecticut carries harsher sentences than in most other states. The sale of narcotic-type drugs and cannabis-type drugs involve the imposition of penalties which differ from offenses involving other controlled drugs. The penalties imposed for offenses involving the hallucinogens, amphetamines and barbiturates are less severe than the penalties imposed for offenses involving the narcotic substances.

Marihuana is not defined as a narcotic drug and a first offense involving possession is not punished as a felony.

Delaware: Del. Code Ann. Tit. 16, Sec. 4701-4732
(Supp. 1968)

Delaware has enacted comprehensive laws aimed at preventing drug abuse. The law reflects the progressive approach of classifying drugs before describing the penalties to be imposed for the varied offenses. Different penalties are imposed for violations involving narcotics, dangerous drugs, and drugs which act as depressants or stimulants upon the central nervous system. These three categories of drugs are classified separately for the purpose of invoking different penalties.

NARCOTIC DRUGS: Narcotic drugs are defined as coca leaves, opium and the opiate derivatives heroin, codeine or any synthetic substitute for these narcotic drugs. The penalties which are invoked for offenses involving narcotic drugs are much more harsh than the penalties invoked for the offenses relating to dangerous drugs and the drugs affecting the central nervous system. It is interesting to note that marihuana is not classified as a narcotic drug.

Possession of a narcotic drug in Delaware is punishable by imprisonment of not more than five years and a fine of not more than $5,000. However, in cases where possession of a narcotic

TABLE X—DELAWARE

Citation	Type of Drug	General Penalty Provisions	Possession	Possession for Sale	Sale and Similar Transactions	Sale to Minor by Adult	Other Offenses
Del. Code Ann. Tit. 16, Sec. 4701-4732 (Supp. 1968)	Narcotic Drugs: (exception to these penalties described in text)		1st: NMT 5 yrs. and NMT $5,000 2nd: 3-10 yrs.	Same as sale	1st: 10-25 yrs. and $5,000-$50,000 fine 2nd: 30-99 yrs.	1st: 15-30 yrs. and fine as Court may determine 2nd: 30 yrs.-99 yrs.	Unlawful manufacture: NMT 10 yrs. and NMT $5,000
	Dangerous Drugs: (exceptions to these penalties described in text)		1st: NMT 2 yrs. and NMT $500 fine 2nd: 2-7 yrs.	Same as sale	1st: 5-10 yrs. and $1,000-$10,000 fine 2nd: 7-15 yrs.	1st: 7-15 yrs. and fine as Court may determine 2nd: 15-25 yrs.	Unlawful manufacture: NMT 5 yrs. and NMT $5,000
	Central Nervous System Depressant or Stimulant Drugs: (exceptions to these penalties described in text)		1st: NMT 2 yrs. and NMT $500 2nd: NLT 2, NMT 7 yrs.	Same as sale	1st: 5-10 yrs. and $1,000-$10,000 fine 2nd: 7-15 yrs.	1st: 7-15 yrs. and fine as Court may determine 2nd: 15-25 yrs.	

1st = 1st offense.
2nd = 2nd offense.
3rd = 3rd offense.
S = Subsequent offense.
NMT = Not more than.
NLT = Not less than.

drug is the offense charged the court may defer prosecution proceedings and place the accused on probation upon reasonable terms and conditions as the court may require. In essence, this provides the first offender who is charged with possession of a narcotic drug the opportunity for another chance to avoid the use of narcotics before any criminal record is acquired. If the probation requirements are complied with, the case is dismissed without any judicial determination of guilt and no criminal record attaches to the accused.

A very strict penalty is imposed for offenses consisting of a sale of a narcotic drug. A first offense is punishable by a sentence of not less than 15 years nor more than 30 years and the defendant may be fined as the court determines. If the defendant has been previously convicted of selling, possessing with intent to sell a narcotic drug or attempt to sell a narcotic drug, the minimum term of imprisonment is 30 years and the maximum term for conviction is 99 years. If a sale of a narcotic drug is made by an adult to a minor, the offense is punishable by imprisonment of 15 to 30 years for a first offender and a sentence of 30 to 99 years for a second offender. It should be clear to the reader that these harsh penalties are presented as deterrents to the use of, sale of, or manufacture of any narcotic drugs.

DANGEROUS DRUGS: The drug abuse laws of Delaware define the dangerous drugs as marihuana, hashish, and any hallucinatory drug including LSD, mescaline, psilocybin, or any drug found by the State Board of Health to have a potential for abuse because of its hallucinatory effect.

The penalties imposed for violations involving the drugs designated as "dangerous drugs" are not as harsh as the laws which impose penalties for offenses involving narcotic drugs. However, in contrast to the legislation of other states, it is apparent that Delaware imposes harsh penalties for offenses involving "dangerous drugs."

Possession of a dangerous drug is punishable by imprisonment of not more than two years and a fine of not more than $500. However, as in offenses involving narcotic drugs, the first offender may be provisionally deferred from prosecution if he complies with probation requirements and, consequently, no criminal penalties attach because there is never a determination of guilt or innocence of the alleged offender.

The unlawful manufacturer of a dangerous drug is punished by imprisonment of not more than five years and not more than $5,000.

The sale of a dangerous drug is punishable by a fine of not less than $1,000 nor more than $10,000 and imprisonment of five to ten years. A second offense is punishable by imprisonment of seven to 15 years.

In situations involving sales, the Delaware statute provides a most interesting approach to the possibility of imposing a harsh sentence upon a person whom the statute is not really aimed at punishing so severely. The purpose of the statute, aimed at preventing sales, is to provide a harsh penalty for those engaged in the sale of dangerous drugs. In order to enable the courts to impose these severe sentences without severely punishing those who are not engaged in selling drugs on a regular basis the penalty is reduced to a fine of $1,000 and/or two years imprisonment if the following mitigating circumstances are proved by the defendant:

1. the defendant is less than 21 years of age, and
2. that the defendant sold a dangerous drug other than a narcotic drug, and
3. that the transaction was an isolated incident as evidenced by the fact that the defendant is not engaged in the business of selling dangerous drugs, and
4. that the sale was made to one who was over 15 years of age and had been acquainted with the defendant for a period of at least one year before any sale took place.

These mitigated penalties apply only in situations where the offense is one involving the sale of a dangerous drug as distinguished from the sale of a narcotic drug.

Mitigated penalties are also designated for the individual charged with possession of a dangerous drug if the accused is able to prove the following elements:

1. that the defendant is under the age of 21 years, and
2. that the defendant did not have in his possession a narcotic drug, and

3. there was no profit involved in obtaining the dangerous drug, and it was obtained with the belief by the defendant that the person who gave him the drug was under 21, and

4. the person the defendant obtained the drug from knew the defendant for a period of one year.

If the above circumstances are presented and proved to the court by the defendant then the ordinary penalty of not more than two years imprisonment and not more than $500 will be reduced to a maximum fined of $500 and/or a maximum of 90 days imprisonment.

Delaware deals uniquely with the problem presented when those who have potential to be rehabilitated commit offenses for which harsh penalties have otherwise been provided. Mitigating the sentence permits the legislature to impose a harsh sentence without unduly hampering the rehabilitative potential of young offenders.

The sale of a dangerous drug by an adult to a minor involves a sentence of seven to 15 years and a fine determined by the court for the first offense. The second offender is presented with a 15 to 25 year sentence.

The unlawful manufacture of dangerous drugs is punishable by imprisonment of not more than five years and a fine of not more than $5,000.

Central Nervous System Depressant or Stimulant Drugs: A separate chapter is devoted to those offenses involving the amphetamines (stimulants) and barbiturates (depressants).

Unlawful possession of amphetamines and barbiturates arises when these drugs are not properly obtained through prescription. Not only is unlawful possession punishable, but unlawful consumption is equally offensive under the statute. Unlawful possession or consumption of depressant or stimulant drugs is punishable by imprisonment of not more than two years and a fine of not more than $500. The second offense is punishable by imprisonment of not less than two nor more than seven years. These penalties are quite severe when contrasted to the higher penalties imposed by other states for cases involving possession of amphetamines or barbiturates.

However mitigating circumstances substantially similar to those circumstances which reduce the penalties imposed where there are offenses involving dangerous drugs may be introduced to lessen the penalty. If these circumstances prevail, the penalty is reduced to a fine of $500 and/or 90 days imprisonment or both.

The burden is upon the defendant to show that he is under 21 years of age, etc. The defendant may establish these mitigating circumstances by presenting the evidence to the jury or he may request a hearing after conviction and present the evidence to the judge prior to sentencing. Unlawful sales of barbiturates and amphetamines carry harsh penalties. The first offender will receive five to ten years imprisonment upon conviction and a fine of $1,000 to $10,000. A second offender will receive a sentence of seven to 15 years.

However, if the defendant can prove the following mitigating circumstances then the penalty is reduced. The following elements must be present:

1. the defendant must be under 21 years of age, and
2. the transaction was an isolated incident as evidenced by the fact that the defendant is not engaged in the business of illegally selling depressant or stimulant drugs, and
3. the sale was made to one who was over 15 years of age and had been acquainted with the defendant for a period of at least one year before any sale took place.

In these instances the maximum penalty is a fine of $1,000 and/ or two years imprisonment. This once more reflects the desire of the legislature to exclude minor transactions among youthful offenders from being treated too severely so as to possibly interfere with the rehabilitative potential of the offender.

These identical mitigating circumstances are available where the sale is made to a minor providing the defendant is under 21. If the mitigating circumstances are not introduced, a sale of a barbiturate or amphetamine drug to a person under 18 years of age is punishable by imprisonment of seven to 15 years and a fine determined by the court for the first offense. The second offense is punishable by imprisonment of 15 to 25 years.

The laws of Delaware which are aimed at preventing drug

TABLE XI—DISTRICT OF COLUMBIA

Citation	Type of Drug	General Penalty Provisions
D.C. Code Ann., Sec. 33-401-425; 33-701-712 (Supp. 1970)	Narcotics	1st: NMT 1 yr. and/or $100 to $1,000 S: NMT 10 yrs. and/or $500 to $5,000
	Amphetamines, Barbiturates and Hallucinogens	1st: NMT 1 yr. and/or NMT $1,000 S: NMT 10 yrs. and NMT $5,000

1st = 1st offense.
2nd = 2nd offense.
3rd = 3rd offense.
S = Subsequent offense.

NMT = Not more than.
NLT = Not less than.

abuse should serve as a model to those states which have not recognized the importance of classifying drugs according to the potential abuse which different substances acquire.

Reducing otherwise harsh penalties in instances where the offender is young and is really not in the regular business of selling drugs illustrates a constructive solution to what otherwise presents a problem when invoking severe penalties for sales offenses.

District of Columbia: D.C. Code Ann., Sec. 33-401-425, 33-701-712 (Supp. 1970)

The laws which attempt to control drug abuse in the District of Columbia appear in one section relating to narcotic drugs and in a separate section directed at other dangerous drugs such as amphetamines, barbiturates and hallucinogens. However, there are similar penalties prescribed for the offenses involving narcotic drugs and dangerous drugs. In the District of Columbia it is unlawful for any person to manufacture, possess, have under his control, sell, prescribe, administer, dispense or compound any narcotic drug.

Blanket penalties are provided for offenses dealing with all types of narcotic drugs and the term "narcotic drug" within the statute includes marihuana. Fertile marihuana seeds have been deemed narcotic drugs within the meaning of the law.

There are only general penalty provisions and there is no specific punishment provided for the sale to a minor by an adult as there is in many other jurisdictions. The general penalty provisions involve a sentence of not more than one year and/or a fine of $100 to $1,000 for the first offense. Subsequent offenses are punishable by imprisonment for not more than ten years and/or a fine of not less than $500 nor more than $5,000.

Florida: Fla. Stat. Ann., Sec. 398.01 et seq. (Supp. 1969). Fla. Stat. Ann., Sec. 404 et seq. (1969)

Florida has adopted the Uniform Narcotic Drug Law. The Uniform Narcotic Drug Law defines narcotic drugs as meaning coca leaves, opium, Isonipecaine®, cannabis, and every substance neither chemically nor physically distinguishable from them,

TABLE XII—FLORIDA

Citation	Type of Drug	General Penalty Provisions	Possession	Possession for Sale	Sale	Sale to Minor
Fla. Stat. Ann., Sec. 398.01 et seq. (Supp. 1969)	Narcotics	1st: 2-5 yrs. and/ or $500-$5,000 2nd: 5-10 yrs. and NMT $10,000 S: 10-20 yrs. and/or NMT $20,000	1st: 2-5 yrs. and/or $500-$5,000 2nd: 5-10 yrs. and/ or NMT $10,000 S: 10-20 yrs. and/or NMT $20,000	1st: NMT 10 yrs. and/or $10,000 2nd: NLT 10 yrs. and NMT 20 yrs. and/or $20,000 S: 20 yrs. to life and/or $20,000	1st: NMT 10 and/or $10,000 2nd: 10-20 yrs. and NMT $20,000 S: 20 yrs. to life and/or $20,000	1st: 10 yrs. to life and NMT $10,000 2nd: 10 yrs. to life and NMT $20,000 S: 20 yrs. to life and NMT $20,000
Fla. Stat. Ann., Sec. 404 et seq. (Supp. 1969)	Amphetamines, Barbiturates, Hallucinogens	1st: NMT 2 yrs. and/or fine of NMT $1,000 2nd: 2-5 yrs. and/or NMT $5,000 S: 5-10 yrs. and/ or $10,000				1st: NMT 10 yrs. or $10,000 S: 5 yrs. to life and NMT $10,000

1st = 1st offense.
2nd = 2nd offense.

3rd = 3rd offense.
S   = Subsequent offense.

NMT = Not more than.
NLT = Not less than.

and any and all derivatives of the same and any other drug to which the narcotics laws of the United States now apply.

Although Florida has not set forth the more specific classifications of drugs such as Delaware has done, offenses involving hallucinogens are equally punishable because the laws now apply to these drugs. In addition, upon publication by the State Board of Health, a drug may be determined to be addiction-forming or addiction sustaining and therefore may be classified as a narcotic drug.

In Florida an additional offense is included in the drug abuse laws which makes it unlawful for any person to possess, have under his control, sell or deliver any device, contrivance, instrument, or paraphenalia with the intent that the device, contrivance, instrument, or paraphenalia be used for unlawfully injecting, smoking, or using any narcotic. Many states have similar statutory provisions.

In contrast to other states, marihuana is classified the same as any other narcotic drug for purposes of invoking penalties.

Georgia: Ga. Code Ann. Sec. 79A-101 to 801, 9901-9916 (Supp. 1969)

Georgia has recognized the need to classify drugs according to the degree to which they are abused. The classification resembles that of Delaware except that in most instances similar penalties are invoked regardless of the nature of the offense. For example the same statutory penalty is set forth for the sale of narcotics as is set forth for the possession of narcotics. In cases involving LSD the possession of this drug involves the same penalty as the sale of the drug. However, it should be apparent that the court will take the type of offense into consideration when determining whether to impose the statutory minimum or the statutory maximum.

The laws of Georgia relating to drug abuse are divided into four separate categories. Offenses can occur where there is possession or sale of the following drugs:

DANGEROUS DRUGS: Possession or sale of these drugs, which are defined as any drug for which a prescription is necessary, is punishable as a misdemeanor.

TABLE XIII—GEORGIA

Citation	Type of Drug	General Penalty Provisions	Addiction	Possession	Possession for Sale	Sale and Similar Transactions	Sale to Minor by Adult
Ga. Code Ann., Sec. 79A-101 to 801, 9901 to 9916 (Supp. 1969)	Narcotics	1st: 2-5 yrs. and a fine of NMT $2,000 2nd: 5-10 yrs. and a fine of NMT $3,000 S: 10-20 yrs. and a fine of NMT $5,000		SEE GENERAL PROVISIONS			
	Dangerous Drugs	Punishable as a misdemeanor		SEE GENERAL PROVISIONS			
	Marihuana, Amphetamines and Barbiturates	1st: NMT 2 yrs. and/or a fine of $2,000 S: NMT 5 yrs. and/or $5,000		SEE GENERAL PROVISIONS			1st: NMT 5 yrs. and/or $5,000 S: NMT 10 yrs. and/or $10,000
	Lysergic Acid Diethylamide (LSD)	1st: 2-5 yrs. and/or $2,000 2nd: 5-10 yrs. and/or $3,000 S: 10-20 yrs. and/or $5,000					

1st = 1st offense.
2nd = 2nd offense.
3rd = 3rd offense.
S = Subsequent offense.

NMT = Not more than.
NLT = Not less than.

NARCOTIC DRUGS: These drugs are defined as coca leaves, opium, Isonipecaine and those substances which are neither chemically nor physically distinguishable from them, and any drug found by the Georgia State Board of Pharmacy to have addiction forming or addiction sustaining liability similar to morphine or cocaine. It is significant to note that marihuana is not classified as a narcotic drug for purposes of invoking the penalties for offenses involving these drugs. Therefore, although this section of the drug abuse laws is referred to as the Uniform Narcotic Drug Act it does differ somewhat from this act in view of the fact that marihuana is not considered a narcotic drug for purposes of invoking legal sanctions. The possession or sale of these drugs is attempted to be controlled by imposing a sentence of two to five years for the first offense and a fine of not more than $2,000. A second offense is treated by imposing a five to ten year sentence and a fine of not more than $3,000. Any subsequent offense is punished by ten to 20 years imprisonment and a fine of not more than $5,000. It is interesting to note that Georgia does not provide any specific provisions which impose a more severe penalty for the sale of a narcotic drug to a minor as most other states do. The penalties described apply to all types of offenses involving these specific drugs.

AMPHETAMINES, BARBITURATES AND MARIHUANA: Offenses which involve abuse of these drugs are embraced in a separate enactment of Georgia's drug abuse laws entitled, *Georgia Drug Abuse Control Act*. This act makes it unlawful to manufacture, sell, deliver, dispose of, or possess any amphetamine, or barbiturate type of drug. It also classifies marihuana with these drugs for purposes of invoking legal sanctions. In addition, the penalties provided in this act also apply to offenses involving any other drug which contains a substance designated by present regulations promulgated under the federal act as having potential for abuse because of its depressant or stimulant effect on the central nervous system or its hallucinogenic effect.

It is important to note that marihuana is classified quite differently in Georgia than it is in many other states. In most states marihuana is separately classified or is grouped with those drugs often classified as narcotic drugs. However, in Georgia, marihuana is grouped with the stimulant and depressant drugs for purposes of invoking penalties. The result is that the possession or sale of marihuana does not involve a sentence as great as offenses involving the narcotic drugs. Possession or sale of the stimulants, depressants or marihuana is punishable by two to five years for the first offense and/or a fine of $2,000. Subsequent offenses are punishable by a fine of not more than five years and/or $5,000. If a sale of these drugs is made to a minor the first offense is punishable by a fine of not more than $5,000 and/or not more than five years imprisonment. Any subsequent offense involving a sale to a minor is punishable by not more than ten years imprisonment and/or $10,000.

LYSERGIC ACID DIETHYLAMIDE (LSD): A provision of the Georgia drug abuse laws prescribes a separate penalty for offenses involving LSD. The penalties invoked for offenses involving this drug are similar to the penalties invoked for offenses involving narcotic drugs. No separate provision is made for invoking a harsher penalty for the sale of LSD to a minor and the same statutory penalty is prescribed for possession as is for the sale of this drug.

This specific provision providing penalties for offenses involving LSD illustrates the response of the legislature to a specific area of drug abuse, because for pharmacological purposes the drug should be classified with those drugs which are described in the *Georgia Drug Abuse Control Act*. This was not practical because the excessive abuse of LSD demanded that greater penalties be designated for offenses involving this drug.

Hawaii: Hawaii Rev. Laws Sec. 329-1 et seq. (1968)

Hawaii has classified the drugs which have potential for abuse into two categories. One chapter entitled, "Narcotics" imposes penalties for the manufacturing, sale, or possession of narcotic drugs. A separate part of the laws, entitled "Drug Abuse Control" is designed to prevent abuse of the amphetamines, barbiturates and hallucinogenic drugs.

Hawaii groups marihuana with narcotics for purposes of imposing penalties for manufacturing, sale or possession. In addition, Hawaii has imposed a penalty for the cultivation of any

TABLE XIV—HAWAII

Citation	Type of Drug	General Penalty Provisions	Possession	Possession for Sale	Sale	Sale to Minor by Adult
Hawaii Rev. Laws Sec. 329-1 et seq. (1968)	Narcotics (including marihuana)	1st: NMT 1 yr. and NMT $1,000 S: NMT 1 yr. and NMT $2,000	1st: NMT 1 yr. and NMT $1,000 S: NMT 1 yr. and NMT $2,000	1st: NMT 10 yrs. and NMT $1,000 S: NMT 20 yrs. and NMT $2,000	1st: NMT 10 yrs. and NMT $1,000 S: NMT 20 yrs. and NMT $2,000	1st: 20 yrs. and NMT $1,000 S: Life and NMT $2,000 No parole until 10 yrs. imprisonment
	Stimulants, Depressants and Hallucinogens		1st: NMT 10 yrs. and NMT $10,000 2nd: NMT 20 yrs. and NMT $20,000	1st: NMT 10 yrs. and NMT $10,000 2nd: NMT 20 yrs. and NMT $20,000	1st: NMT 10 yrs. and NMT $10,000 2nd: NMT 20 yrs. and NMT $20,000	1st: NMT 20 yrs. and NMT $1,000 2nd: Life and NMT $2,000

1st = 1st offense.
2nd = 2nd offense.
3rd = 3rd offense.
S = Subsequent offense.
NMT = Not more than.
NLT = Not less than.

TABLE XV IDAHO

Citation	Type of Drug	Unlawful Manufacture, Unlawful Distribution, Possession With Intent to Distribute	Possession	Non-compliance with Registration Requirements	Sale to a Minor
Idaho Code Ann., Sec. 37-2701 et seq. (1969)	Schedule I 42 Opiates, 22 Opium derivates, 17 Hallucinogens	Narcotic: NMT 15 yrs. and/or NMT $25,000 Non-narcotic: NMT 5 yrs. and/or NMT $15,000 or both S. Up to twice the penalty for 1st.	Punished as a misdemeanor	NMT 1 yr. and/or NMT $25,000 S. Twice penalty for 1st.	Maximum of twice the penalty prescribed for ordinary sale.
	Schedule II Opium, opiate, opium poppy, & straw, coca leaves and 21 specific opiates	Narcotic: NMT 15 yrs. and/or NMT $25,000 Non-narcotic: NMT 5 yrs. and/or NMT $15,000 S: Up to twice the penalty for 1st.	Punished as a misdemeanor	NMT 1 yr. and/or NMT $25,000 S: Twice penalty for 1st.	Maximum of twice the penalty prescribed for ordinary sale.
	Schedule III Amphetamine, phenmetrazine, methylphenizate, and barbiturates	NMT 5 yrs. and/or NMT $15,000 S: Up to twice the penalty for 1st.	Punished as a misdemeanor	NMT 1 yr. and/or NMT $25,000 S: Twice penalty for 1st.	Maximum of twice the penalty prescribed for ordinary sale.
	Schedule IV 11 specific barbiturates	NMT 3 yrs. and/or NMT $10,000 S: Up to twice the penalty for 1st.	Punished as a misdemeanor	NMT 1 yr. and/or NMT $25,000 S: Twice penalty for 1st.	Maximum of twice the penalty prescribed for ordinary sale.
	Schedule V Compounds and mixtures containing small amounts of narcotic substances	NMT 1 yr. and/or $1,000 S: Up to twice penalty for 1st.	Punished as a misdemeanor	NMT 1 yr. and/or NMT $25,000 S: Twice penalty for 1st.	Maximum of twice the penalty prescribed for ordinary sale.

1st = 1st offense.
2nd = 2nd offense.

3rd = 3rd offense.
S = Subsequent offense.

NMT = Not more than.
NLT = Not less than.

narcotic. Under this provision a person who knowingly plants, cultivates, produces or manufactures any narcotic drugs, is, upon conviction, punished by not more than five years imprisonment for the first offense and not more than ten years for the second offense.

Stimulants, depressants and hallucinogens such as LSD, peyote and psilocybin, amphetamines and barbiturates are grouped together for purposes of providing penalties for offenses involving these drugs. The possession and sale of these drugs involve similar penalties. However sale of these drugs to a minor or inducing a minor to use these drugs is treated more harshly. The punishment in these instances is not more than 20 years and a fine of not more than $1,000 for the first offense and life imprisonment and not more than a $2,000 fine for a subsequent offense.

The drug abuse laws of Hawaii reflect a strong effort on the part of the legislature to severely punish those who are convicted of selling drugs to minors.

Idaho: Idaho Code Ann. Sec. 37-2701 et seq. (1969)

Idaho has recently adopted the Uniform Controlled Substances Act. All dangerous drugs with a potential for abuse are classified under five schedules and penalties imposed for offenses depend upon the schedule in which the drug is grouped.

The provisions for conditional discharge of criminal charges for first offenses involving possession are adopted from the federal act. However, the provision which allows the records of minors to be expunged under federal law does not appear in the Idaho statute.

Illinois: Ill. Stat. Ann. Ch. 38 Sec. 22-1 and Ch. 111 ½
Sec. 801 (Supp. 1970)

In Illinois the laws directed at preventing drug abuse are embraced in two distinct statutes. The laws relating to narcotics are separated from the laws directed at preventing the abuse of stimulant, depressant, and hallucinogenic drugs.

A provision of the narcotic law makes it a crime to use nar-

TABLE XVI—ILLINOIS

Citation	Type of Drug	General Penalty Provisions	Addiction	Possession	Sale and Similar Transaction	Sale to Minor by Adult	Other Offenses
Illinois Stat. Ann. Ch. 38 Sec. 22-1 and Ch. 111½ Sec. 801 (Supp. 1970)	Narcotics		NLT 90 days, NMT 1 yr., probation NMT 5 yrs.	1st: NMT $5,000 and 2-10 yrs. S: 5 yrs. to life	1st: 10 yrs. to life S: life with no probation or suspension		Inducing Minor: 2-5 yrs. Mfg. and Compound drugs: NMT $5,000 and 2-10 yrs. with no probation or suspension. Professional compliance: 1st: NMT $1,000 and/or 1 yr. S: NMT $3,000 and/or 5 yrs.
	Marihuana			1st: NMT 1 yr. and/or $1,500 S: 2-10 yrs. and/or NMT $5,000			
	Stimulant, depressant, and hallucinogens	1st: $100-$1,000 and/or 1 yr. S: $500-$2,500 and/or 1-5 yrs.				1st: NMT $5,000 and/or NLT 2 yrs. S: NLT $15,000 and/or 5-6 yrs.	

1st = 1st offense.
2nd = 2nd offense.

3rd = 3rd offense.
S = Subsequent offense.

NMT = Not more than.
NLT = Not less than.

cotics. In addition it is further provided that multiple punctures on body surfaces or scars or abrasions resulting from hypodermic needle punctures are prima facie evidence of the repeated unlawful use of narcotic drugs. A conviction under this section makes it mandatory that the violator be confined for at least 90 days. In addition, the violator may be placed on probation for not more than five years.

Possession of narcotic drugs is punishable by a fine of not more than $5,000 and two to ten years imprisonment for the first offense. A subsequent offense is punishable by five years to life imprisonment.

Although marihuana is classified as a narcotic drug in Illinois for purposes of imposing penalties, the *possession* of marihuana is treated separately for purposes of invoking punishment. The legislature has exempted this drug from the harsher penalties involved in the possession of the opiate derivatives such as heroin. The possession of marihuana is punishable by imprisonment of not more than one year and/or a fine of $1,500 for the first offense. Any subsequent offense involving the possession of marihuana is punishable by a fine of not more than $5,000 and two to ten years imprisonment.

Offenses involving stimulants, depressants and hallucinogenic substances are treated separately in the Drug Abuse Control Act. The act became effective January 1, 1968 for the purpose of controlling the manufacture, distribution, delivery and possession of depressant, stimulant or hallucinogenic drugs. The penalties are provided for in general provisions which treat all offenses similarly with the exception of a sale of these drugs to a minor. The general penalty provisions provide for fines of $100 to $1,000 and/or one year imprisonment for the first offense. Subsequent offenses are punishable by a fine of $500 to $2,500 and/or imprisonment of one to five years.

A sale to a minor is punishable by not less than two years imprisonment and/or a fine of $5,000. A subsequent offense is punishable by a fine of not less than $15,000 and/or imprisonment of five to six years.

*Indiana: Ind. Stat. Ann., Sec. 10-3501 et seq. (Supp. 1970);
Ind. Stat. Ann. Sec. 35-3332 et seq. (Supp. 1970)*

The problem of drug abuse in Indiana has been attacked by two separate acts. The Narcotic Drug Act is aimed at preventing the abuse of narcotic drugs. Marihuana is classified within this group for purposes of imposing penalties. A separate act entitled, the *Indiana Dangerous Drug Act* prevents the abuse of *all dangerous drugs*. Under the prior Dangerous Drug Act only the abuse of amphetamines and barbiturates was prohibited by law. Ostensibly, the legislature of Indiana recognized that the abuse of other drugs, such as hallucinogenic drugs, required that the statute be amended. Under the present Dangerous Drug Act there is extensive prohibition of drugs which are not classified as narcotic drugs. These provisions are more comprehensive than those preventing the manufacture, sale or possession of dangerous drugs in other states because there is a more significant definition of the words "dangerous drugs."

Dangerous drug, for purposes of this act, means "(1) any drug the label of which is required by federal law to bear the statement: 'caution: federal law prohibits dispensing without a prescription'; (2) any drug which, because of its toxicity or other potentiality for harmful effect, or the method of its use, or the collateral measures necessary to its use, is not safe for use except under the supervision of a practitioner licensed by law to prescribe or administer such drug; (3) a new drug which is limited by an effective application under state law to use under the professional supervision of a practitioner licensed by law to prescribe or administer such drug; (4) any hallucinogenic, psychedelic, psychotogenic drug or substance including but not limited to lysergic acid diethylamide, commonly known as LSD; or (5) any drug appearing on the consolidated list of DACA drugs compiled in compliance with the drug abuse control amendments," of the federal law.

Therefore, in Indiana, dangerous drug legislation relates not only to the amphetamines, barbiturates, and hallucinogenic drugs but to any drug which has a potential for abuse and ap-

TABLE XVII—INDIANA

Citation	Type of Drug	General Penalty Provisions	Possession	Possession for Sale	Sale and Similar Transactions	Sale to Minor
Ind. Stat. Ann., Sec. 10-3501 et seq. (Supp. 1970) Sec. 35-3332 et seq. (Supp. 1970)	Narcotics (including marihuana)	1-5 yrs. and/or NMT $1,000	1st: 2-10 yrs. and NMT $1,000 S: 5-20 yrs. and NMT $2,000	1st: 5-20 yrs. and NMT $2,000 S: 20 yrs. to life and NMT $5,000	1st: NMT $2,000 and NLT 5-20 yrs. S: 20 yrs. to life and NMT $5,000	
	All Other Drugs with Potential for Abuse	1st: 1-10 yrs. and NMT $1,000 S: 2-15 yrs. and NMT $3,000	Same as General Penalty Provisions	Same as General Penalty Provisions	Same as General Penalty Provisions	Same as General Penalty Provisions

1st = 1st offense.
2nd = 2nd offense.

3rd = 3rd offense.
S = Subsequent offense.

NMT = Not more than.
NLT = Not less than.

pears on the comprehensive list of drugs regulated by federal law, and any other drug which is required by law to be dispensed by prescription or through a person licensed to practice medicine. All offenses involving these drugs come within the purview of the same statute which provides for penalties of not less than one year nor more than ten years and a fine not to exceed $1,000 for the first offense. A subsequent offense is punishable by imprisonment of not less than two nor more than 15 years. Undoubtedly, the penalty does have a wide range and the punishment imposed would invariably depend upon whether the offense involved the sale or possession of dangerous drugs.

The Indiana Dangerous Drug Act also provides that "any store, shop, warehouse, dwelling house, apartment building, vehicle, boat, aircraft, or any place whatever, which is used by any person for the purpose of illegally keeping or selling any dangerous drug" shall be deemed a common nuisance. Any person who keeps or maintains such a place is subsequent to a fine of $25 to $100 and may be imprisoned for a period of not more than six months. Many other states have enacted similar provisions.

The statutes providing penalties for offenses involving violations of narcotic drugs, as distinguished from those classified as dangerous drugs, contain a provision which declares that a drug addict is dangerous in public places and is subject to three months confinement and a fine of $300. He is also prohibited from entering public places, including streets and highways, unless he can present positive proof that he is under the care of a licensed physician for the treatment of addiction.

In contrast to many of the other states, the Indiana law relating to narcotic drugs does not specifically include an increased penalty for the sale of a narcotic drug or dangerous drug to a minor. However, the sentencing authority probably takes this into consideration when deciding upon the sentence to be imposed.

It is interesting to note that the provisions for penalties involving offenses related to narcotic drugs appear in the criminal law sections of the statutes but the provisions for penalties for offenses involving dangerous drugs appear in the Health Code section of the statutes.

Iowa: Iowa Code Ann., Sec. 204-1 et seq. (Supp. 1970)

Iowa has enacted two separate acts which attempt to curb drug abuse. The provisions which set forth the penalties for the illegal sale or possession of narcotic drugs in Iowa are substantially similar to the provisions of most other states which have adopted the Uniform Narcotic Drug Act.

Iowa has relaxed the penalties imposed in cases involving a first offense of possession of marihuana. In the section of the statute which provides the penalties for offenses involving narcotic drugs, a recent amendment states that if a person violates the law by possessing, purchasing, or attempting to purchase marihuana in such quantity that it can logically be inferred that the marihuana is intended for personal use then the accused shall be guilty of possession of marihuana for personal use and upon a first conviction shall be imprisoned in the county jail for not more than six months *or* receive a fine of not more than $1,000. In addition the court may suspend all or part of the sentence or probation may be granted if the court determines that a recurrence of a violation of the chapter is unlikely.

However, if the marihuana is purchased with the idea of subsequently selling it to others then the offender is punished by the same penalty prescribed for offenses involving other narcotic drugs. A second offense for possession for personal use is treated harshly. The statute states that the second offense for possession for personal use is punishable by two to five years imprisonment and a fine of not more than $2,000. This is similar to the penalties invoked for first offenses involving the more dangerous narcotics such as heroin and other opiates. In essence, Iowa has carved an exception out of the harsh penalties which apply to offenses involving narcotic drugs in instances involving possession of marihuana if it can logically be inferred that it is for personal use and not possessed for purposes of sale.

A separate chapter of the laws of Iowa delineates those offenses involving depressant, stimulant, and hallucinogenic drugs.

The sale or possession of these drugs is punishable by a fine

TABLE XVIII—IOWA

Citation	Type of Drug	General Penalty Provisions	Addiction	Possession	Possession for Sale	Sale	Sale to Minor by Adult
Iowa Code Ann., Sec. 204-1 et seq. (Supp. 1970)	Narcotics (not including marihuana)	1st: 2-5 yrs. and NMT $2,000 2nd: 5-10 yrs. and NMT $2,000 S: 10-20 yrs. and NMT $2,000	Treatment until cured				1st and S: 5-20 yrs.
	Marihuana			Possession for Personal Use: 1st: NMT $1,000 or 6 mos. with possible suspended sentence 2nd: 2-5 yrs. and NMT $2,000	1st: 2-5 yrs. and NMT $2,000 2nd: 5-10 yrs. and NMT $2,000 S: 10-20 yrs. and NMT $2,000	Same as Possession for Sale	1st and S: 5-20 yrs.
	Stimulants, Depressants and Hallucinogens	1st: NMT 1 yr. and/or $1,000 S: NMT 5 yrs. and/or $2,000		Same as General Penalty Provisions	Same as General Penalty Provisions	Same as General Penalty Provisions	1st: NMT $2,000 and/or 5 yrs. S: $5,000 and/or 20 yrs.

1st = 1st offense.
2nd = 2nd offense.
3rd = 3rd offense.
S = Subsequent offense.
NMT = Not more than.
NLT = Not less than.

of $1,000 or imprisonment for not more than one year if the drugs were obtained without a prescription. Subsequent offenses are punishable by a fine of not more than $2,000 and/or imprisonment in the penitentiary for not more than five years. However, the sale to a minor is treated more harshly. The first offense of a sale involving one of the enumerated depressant, stimulant or hallucinogenic drugs is punishable by a fine of not more than $2,000 or imprisonment in the penitentiary for not more than five years. Subsequent offenses are punishable by a fine of not more than $5,000 and/or not more than 20 years in prison. It is interesting to note that the penalties for illegal possession of amphetamines, barbiturates or hallucinogens are more severe than they are for offenses involving the possession of marihuana for personal use.

Kansas: Kan. Stat. Ann., Sec. 65-2501 et seq. (1964);
Kan. Stat. Ann., Sec. 65-2519(b) (1964); Kan. Stat. Ann.,
Sec. 65-2601 et seq. (1964)

Kansas has enacted a Uniform Narcotic Drug Act which regulates activities involving narcotic drugs. In addition, as in most other states, it was necessary to enact separate laws relating to the manufacture, sale or possession of all other dangerous drugs.

Narcotic drugs, for purposes of imposing penalties for offenses involving these substances, includes "coca leaves, opium, cannabis, Isonipecaine, Amidone®, isoamidone, ketobemidone and every other substance neither chemically nor physically distinguishable from them; any other drugs to which the federal narcotic laws now apply, and any drug found by the state board of pharmacy and the state board of health, after reasonable notice and opportunity for hearing, to have an addiction-forming or addiction-sustaining liability similar to morphine or cocaine, from the effective date of determination of such finding by state board of pharmacy and state board of health." In Kansas, it is unlawful for any person to manufacture, possess, have under his control, sell, prescribe, administer, dispense or compound any narcotic drug, except as authorized. The authorization extends to physicians, veterinarians and pharmacists. The physicians and pharmacists are required to comply with the statutory regulations which provide for specific written orders and recording procedures. A physician, veterinarian or pharmacist who violates any of the mandatory requirements is guilty of a class A misdemeanor which is punishable by confinement in the county jail for not more than one year and/or a fine of not more than $2,500.

Any other individual who manufactures, possesses or sells narcotic drugs is guilty of a class D felony. In Kansas a class D felony is punishable by an indeterminate term of imprisonment, the minimum of which shall be fixed by the court at not less than one year nor more than three years and a maximum of no more than ten years.

It is interesting to note that the Kansas statute does not *specifically* provide different penalties for the offenses involving narcotic drugs as most other states do. In many other states possession is treated less harshly than sale of narcotic drugs. A further analysis of most states indicates a more severe penalty is provided if the sale of a narcotic drug is to a minor. However, the laws of Kansas punish the manufacture, sale or possession of narcotics by classifying all of these offenses as class D felonies and providing penalties accordingly. Of course, the court does exercise discretion when imposing sentence and undoubtedly considers the gravity of the offense before deciding whether to impose a minimum or maximum sentence.

One distinctive provision of the Uniform Narcotic Drug Act of Kansas seems to encourage larger cities within the state of Kansas to adopt ordinances for the purposes of controlling traffic in narcotic drugs within their corporate limits. Ostensibly, this significant provision attempts to attack drug abuse at a local level.

One recent amendment reflects the growing trend to reduce the penalties for possession of marihuana if the possession is for personal use as distinguished from possession for purposes of selling. This recent amendment states that any person possessing marihuana for personal use in violation of the Uniform Narcotic Drug Act is guilty of a class A misdemeanor. In essence this means the legislature has carved an exception out of the blanket-type punishments for violations of the laws relating to

TABLE XIX—KANSAS

Citation	Type of Drug	General Penalty Provisions	Possession	Possession for Sale	Sale and Similar Transactions	Sale to Minor by Adult	Other Offenses
Kan. Stat. Ann., Sec. 65-2501 et seq. (1964)	Narcotics (not including marihuana)	*Class D Felony:* Indeterminate sentence but court sets minimum at 1 to 3 yrs. and the maximum at 10 yrs.					
Kan. Stat. Ann., Sec. 65-2519(b) (1964)	Marihuana		*Class A Misdemeanor:* 1st: NMT 1 yr. and/or NMT $2,500 2nd: Treated same as General Penalty Provisions for Narcotic drugs (Class D Felony)	*Class D Felony:* Indeterminate sentence with minimum set by court at 1-3 yrs. and maximum of 10 yrs.	*Class D Felony:* Same as Possession for Sale	Same	

| Kan. Stat. Ann., Sec. 65-2601 et seq. (1964) | Dangerous drugs (amphetamines, barbiturates and hallucinogens) | 1st: Class A misdemeanor punishable by NMT 1 yr. and/or NMT $2,500 2nd: Class D Felony indeterminate sentence, 1-3 yrs. minimum set by court with maximum NMT 10 yrs. | 1st: Class C Felony Indeterminate sentence, 1-5 yrs. minimum set by court with maximum NMT 20 yrs. and/or $10,000 2nd: Class B Felony Indeterminate sentence with minimum set by court at 5 to 15 yrs. and maximum of life imprisonment 3rd: Class A Felony Life imprisonment | Same | Same |

1st = 1st offense.
2nd = 2nd offense.

3rd = 3rd offense.
S = Subsequent offense.

NMT = Not more than.
NLT = Not less than.

narcotic drugs because a class A misdemeanor is punishable by confinement in the county jail for not more than one year and/ or a fine of not more than $2,500. However, if the possession is with intent to sell or if there is a second offense of possession of marihuana for personal use then the defendant is guilty of a class D felony and is punished accordingly. There are no provisions which specifically set forth harsher penalties for second offenders.

A separate act prohibits the manufacture, delivery (including sale) or possession of all other dangerous drugs. For purposes of this act a "drug" includes the amphetamines, barbiturates, hallucinogens and all other drugs which are considered by the state board of health "to have a dangerous hallucinogenic, hypnotic, somnifacient or stimulating effect on the body of a human or animal." As used in this act, a "dangerous drug" includes those drugs which are unsafe for use except under the supervision of a practitioner because of its toxicity or other potentiality for human effect. The act makes it unlawful to possess or deliver any of these dangerous drugs unless prescribed by a physician and administered by a pharmacist in accordance with the statutory mandates relating to written orders and prescriptions for these drugs. Any violations are considered class A misdemeanors and are punishable by not more than one year confinement in the county jail and/or a fine of not more than $2,500.

The penalties invoked for offenses involving narcotic drugs differ from the provisions for penalties involving dangerous drugs. For offenses involving dangerous drugs increased penalties are *specifically* provided for. A second offense involving dangerous drugs is considered a class D felony. This requires a minimum punishment of one to three years and a maximum of not more than ten years. The above punishments are imposed upon those pharmacists and other persons who do not comply with the legal requirements set forth for obtaining these drugs. A recent amendment to the section dealing with hallucinogenic drugs imposes a harsher punishment for those persons engaged in the illegal sale of hallucinogenic or stimulating drugs described in the act. These punishments are harsher than some of those imposed for offenses involving narcotic drugs under the Kansas Uniform

Narcotic Drug Act. A first offense involving the sale, offer for sale, or possession with intent to sell is punishable by a minimum of one to five years and a maximum of 20 years and/or a fine of $10,000. A second offense is considered a Class B felony and is punishable by imprisonment of a minimum of five to 15 years and a maximum of life and/or a fine of $10,000. A third or subsequent offense involving the sale, attempted sale or possession with intent to sell these dangerous drugs is punishable by life imprisonment.

Kentucky: Ky. Rev. Stat. Ann. 217 et seq. (Supp. 1970)

Kentucky provides very strict penalties for violations of the narcotic laws. The first offense involving possession of a narcotic drug is punishable by two to ten years imprisonment and a fine of not more than $20,000. Each subsequent offense is punishable by imprisonment of five to 20 years and a fine of not more than $20,000. In addition, a separate provision states that any person who uses, or who is under the influence of a narcotic drug within the Commonwealth of Kentucky, other than for legitimate medical treatment administered or prescribed by a doctor, shall be confined in the county jail for 12 months. The court, after conviction, may place the defendant on probation provided the defendant consents to enter, and does enter, an institution approved by the court for treatment of such condition and remains therein until discharged by said institution. If the defendant fails to stay in the institution until he is released, then his probation is automatically revoked and he must serve his sentence in the county jail.

The sale of a narcotic drug to a minor by an adult is punished harshly and involves a sentence of twenty years to life and a fine of not more than $20,000.

Although Kentucky adopted the Uniform Narcotic Drug Act, marihuana has recently been excluded from the list of narcotic drugs which involve severe penalties. Under the recent amendment marihuana is now considered a dangerous drug and is categorized with the stimulants, depressants and hallucinogens. The manufacture, sale or fraudulent procurement of any of these drugs is punishable by not more than five years and/or a fine of

TABLE XX—KENTUCKY

Citation	Type of Drug	General Penalty Provisions	Possession	Sale to Minor by Adult
Ky. Rev. Stat. Ann. Sec. 218 et seq. (Supp. 1970)	Narcotics	1st: 5-20 yrs. and NMT $20,000 S: 10-40 yrs. and NMT $20,000	1st: 2-10 yrs. and NMT $20,000 S: 5-20 yrs. and NMT $20,000	20 yrs. to life and NMT $20,000
Ky. Rev. Stat. Ann. Sec. 217 et seq. (Supp. 1970)	Marihuana and other Dangerous Drugs	1st: NMT 5 yrs. and/or $5,000 S: NMT 10 yrs. and/or $10,000	1st: 1 yr. of rehabilitation program or 6 mos. or $600 2nd: 1 yr. and/or $1,000 S: NMT 5 yrs. and/or $5,000	1st: NMT 10 yrs. and/or $20,000 S: NMT 20 yrs. and/or $20,000

1st = 1st offense.
2nd = 2nd offense.
3rd = 3rd offense.
S = Subsequent offense.

NMT = Not more than.
NLT = Not less than.

$5,000 for the first offense and not more than ten years and/or $10,000 for the second offense. The sale of dangerous drugs to a minor is punished by a term of imprisonment twice that authorized for sales to adults.

Kentucky has taken a progressive approach in dealing with offenses involving *possession* of dangerous drugs. If the possession is for the personal use of the accused then the offense is treated as a misdemeanor. (This includes offenses involving possession of marihuana for personal use.) Upon conviction the individual is ordered to a designated facility for a program of rehabilitation and treatment. The person has five days after sentencing to appear at the facility. The director of the facility has the power to notify the sentencing court if the person is unwilling to participate in the rehabilitation program. If the director notifies the court of this fact, the court may order the person to cooperate with the rehabilitation program or it may impose a fine of $600 and/or confinement in county jail for not more than six months. A second offense involving possession of the dangerous drugs is treated as a misdemeanor and upon conviction is punishable by confinement in the county jail for not more than one year or by a fine of not more than $1,000 or both. Subsequent offenses are punished by confinement in the penitentiary for not more than five years and a fine of $5,000. However, even in cases involving second offenses and subsequent offenses, the court is given the power to impose a sentence of probation if the person becomes involved in a program offered by a rehabilitative facility.

It is most important to note the provision of the Kentucky statutes relating to dangerous drugs which provides that a person who is convicted for the first time of possession of a dangerous drug (including marihuana) can have his conviction set aside upon satisfactory completion of treatment, probation or other sentence. A certificate is issued by the court to this effect and a conviction which is voided under this subsection of the statute is not regarded as a conviction for purposes of disqualifications or disabilities imposed by law upon conviction of a crime. In essence this means that if a person is convicted of possessing marihuana, barbiturates, amphetamines or hallucinogenic drugs for personal use, he can serve his sentence by cooperating in a program which will attempt to rehabilitate him and upon completion of this treatment his "criminal" record is expunged.

Louisiana: La. Rev. Stat. Ann., Sec. 40:963 (1970)

Louisiana has enacted a *Uniform Controlled Dangerous Substances Law* which supersedes the *Uniform Narcotic Drug Law*. The new act has listed all the controlled substances, and much like the new *Federal Drug Abuse Prevention and Control Act of 1970*, classifies these substances according to their potentiality for abuse, the scientific evidence of its pharmacological effect, the state of current scientific knowledge regarding the substance and its psychic or physiological dependence liability. After the State Board of Health considers the factors mentioned above, a controlled substance is classified under one of four schedules. The penalties imposed for violations involving these substances depends on which of the four schedules the drug is grouped in. For example, Schedule I contains three groups of drugs. The first group are a list of 42 dangerous substances. The second group classified in Schedule I includes the opium derivatives including heroin, codeine, nicocodeine, morphine, and other opium derivatives. The third group of drugs under Schedule I includes marihuana, peyote, psilocybin, tetrahydrocannabinol, mescaline, LSD and other hallucinogens. It is interesting to note that marihuana is classified with the drugs defined as hallucinogenic substances. This step toward reclassifying marihuana is similar to the reclassification by the federal government under the *Drug Abuse Prevention and Control Act of 1970*. This classification of Schedule I substances is based on the fact that these drugs have no currently accepted medical use.

Under Schedule II the Board of Health of the State of Louisiana classified those drugs which have:

1. a high potential for abuse; and
2. currently accepted medical use in the United States, or currently accepted medical use with severe restrictions; and
3. abuse may lead to severe psychic or physical dependence or disorders.

The drugs included under Schedule II include:

TABLE XLII—LOUISIANA

Citation	Type of Drug	Unlawful Manufacture, Unlawful Distribution, Possession With Intent to Distribute	Unlawful Possession	Sale or Distribution to a Minor
La. Rev. Stat. Ann Sec. 40:963 (1970) Uniform Controlled Dangerous Substance Law	*Schedule I* (a) 42 dangerous substances (b) 17 opium derivatives (including Heroin) (c) 12 Hallucinogens (including Marihuana)	If a narcotic drug, NMT 30 yrs. and/or NMT $15,000 If a non-narcotic drug, NMT 10 yrs. and/or NMT $15,000 S: Twice the penalty authorized for 1st.	NMT 5 yrs. and/or $5,000 *Except Marihuana:* 1st: NMT 1 yr. and/or $500 2nd: NMT 5 yrs. and/or $2,000 3rd: NMT 20 yrs. with no benefits of parole, probation or suspended sentence	Twice the penalty authorized for ordinary sale
	Schedule II (a) opium, coca leaves and opiate and all derivatives chemically equivalent (b) 20 opiates	Narcotic Drugs: NMT 30 yrs. and/or NMT $15,000 Non-Narcotic Drugs: NMT 10 yrs. and/or NMT $15,000 S: Twice the penalty authorized for 1st.	NMT 5 yrs. and/or $5,000 S: Twice the penalty authorized for 1st.	Twice the penalty authorized for ordinary sale
	Schedule III (a) amphetamines (b) barbiturates (c) mixtures containing small amounts of narcotic drugs if combined with non-narcotic ingredients	NMT 10 yrs. and/or NMT $15,000 S: Twice the penalty authorized for 1st.	NMT 5 yrs. and/or $5,000 S: Twice the penalty authorized for 1st.	Twice the penalty authorized for ordinary sale
	Schedule IV Mixtures containing small amounts of Codeine	NMT 5 yrs. and/or $5,000 S: Twice the penalty authorized for 1st.	NMT 5 yrs. and/or $5,000 S: Twice the penalty authorized for 1st.	Twice the penalty authorized for ordinary sale

1st = 1st offense.
2nd = 2nd offense.

3rd = 3rd offense.
S = Subsequent offense.

NMT = Not more than.
NLT = Not less than.

1. opium, coca leaves and opiate, and
2. any salt, compound, derivative or preparation of opium, coca leaves or opiate, and
3. any salt or compound which is chemically equivalent to the substance referred to in (1) and (2) above, and
4. opium, poppy and poppy straw.

In addition, 20 opiates are included within Schedule II.

Under Schedule III, the State Board of Health of Louisiana classifies those drugs which have:

1. a potential for abuse less than the substance listed in Schedules I and II, and
2. well-documented and approved medical use in the United States, and
3. abuse may lead to moderate or low physical dependence or high psychological dependence.

This category invariably includes the amphetamines and barbiturates or other drugs which have a tendency to depress or stimulate the central nervous system. It also includes eight compounds, mixtures or preparations containing limited quantities of narcotic drugs combined with equal or greater quantities of non-narcotic ingredients in therapeutic amounts.

Schedule IV includes substances which the Louisiana State Board of Health finds to have:

1. a low potential for abuse relative to the substances listed in Schedule III, and
2. currently accepted medical use in the United States, and
3. limited physical dependence and/or psychological dependence liability relative to the substances listed in Schedule III.

Included within Schedule IV are compounds, mixtures and preparations which contain limited quantities of narcotic drugs and one or more non-narcotic active medical ingredients in sufficient proportion to confer upon the compound or preparation valuable medicinal qualities.

The manufacture or possession with intent to distribute or the distribution of any drug within Schedule I or II which is a narcotic drug is punishable by imprisonment of not more than 30 years and/or a fine of not more than $15,000. If the offense involves a non-narcotic drug, then the possession involves a penalty of imprisonment not to exceed ten years and/or a fine of not more than $15,000.

For offenses involving the unlawful manufacture, possession with intent to distribute or distribution of dangerous substances included in Schedule III, which include the barbiturates and amphetamines, the offender may be imprisoned for not more than ten years and/or may be fined not more than $1,500. The unlawful manufacture, possession with intent to distribute and distribution of dangerous substances which are classified under Schedule IV is punishable by not more than five years imprisonment and/or $5,000. For offenses involving unlawful manufacture or distribution the consideration is not only what schedule the drug is classified under but whether it is a narcotic drug. The statute defines a narcotic drug as:

> [A]ny of the following, whether produced directly or indirectly by extraction from substances of vegetable origin or independently by means of chemical synthesis, or by a combination of extraction and chemical synthesis:
> (a) Opium, coca leaves, and opiates;
> (b) A compound manufacture, salt derivative or preparation of opium, coca leaves, or opiates;
> (c) A substance and any compound, manufacture, salt derivative, or preparation thereof which is chemically identical with any of the substances referred to in clauses (a) and (b).

"Opiate" is defined as "any dangerous substance having an addiction forming or addiction sustaining liability similar to morphine or being capable of conversion into a drug having such addiction forming or addiction sustaining liability."

Possession of all the dangerous substances is treated uniformly by providing for similar penalties for drugs falling under all four schedules. An exception is made for offenses involving possession of marihuana.

Unlawful possession of any dangerous substance (except marihuana) is punishable by a term of imprisonment not to exceed five years and/or a fine of $5,000. For offenses involving possession of marihuana the penalties are much less severe. A first offense involving possession of marihuana is punished as a misdemeanor and the offender is subject to a fine of $500 and/or imprisonment in the parish jail for not more than one year. A second offender is subject to a fine of $2,000 and/or imprisonment of not more than five years. A third or subsequent offense involving the possession of marihuana involves imprisonment of not more than 20 years without any benefits of parole, probation or suspension of sentence. Analysis of the provisions relating to penalties indicates that a person unlawfully obtaining barbiturates or amphetamines (obtaining these drugs other than by prescription) is punished for this unlawful possession much more severely than an individual convicted the first time for unlawful possession of marihuana. These penalty provisions prevail despite the fact that the statute itself recognizes that marihuana has no currently acceptable medical use in the United States and the barbiturates and amphetamines do have a currently accepted medical use in the United States.

The statute provides sentences which are twice as harsh for all second offenders and for the sale of any controlled substance to minors.

Maine: Me. Rev. Stat. Ann. Tit. 22, Sec. 2361 (Supp. 1970)

The recent amendments to the laws relating to drug abuse in Maine reflect the growing trend to take marihuana out of the category of narcotics for purposes of imposing a penalty.

In dealing with the problems represented by possession of marihuana, Maine amended the laws relating to drug abuse and removed marihuana from the section of drugs defined as narcotics. This enabled the legislature to enact a separate law governing the possession and sale of marihuana and peyote. A first offense for possession of marihuana is punished as a misdemeanor with a sentence of not more than 11 months and a fine of not more than $1,000. Subsequent offenses involving the possession of marihuana involve penalties of not more than two years imprisonment and a fine of not more than $2,000. The sale of marihuana or peyote is punishable by imprisonment of not less than one nor more than five years in prison.

TABLE XXII—MAINE

Citation	Type of Drug	General Penalty Provisions	Possession	Sale	Sale to Minor by Adult	Other Offenses
Me. Rev. Stat. Ann. Tit. 22, Sec. 2361 (Supp. 1970)	Narcotics and Hallucinatory Drugs	1st: 2-8 yrs. and NMT $1,000 2nd: 5-15 yrs. and NMT $2,000 S: 10-20 yrs. and NMT $5,000			NMT 20 yrs. and NMT $10,000	
	Barbiturates and Amphetamines	NMT 6 mos. and/or $1,000				
	Marihuana and Peyote		1st: NMT $1,000 and NMT 11 mos. S: NMT 2 yrs. and NMT $2,000	1-5 yrs.	If minor is 18-20: 2-6 yrs. If minor is under 18: 1st: 3-8 yrs. S: 4-10 yrs. If seller is under 21: NMT 5 yrs.	Knowingly in presence of person in possession: NMT $1,000 and 11 mos.

1st = 1st offense.
2nd = 2nd offense.

3rd = 3rd offense.
S = Subsequent offense.

NMT = Not more than.
NLT = Not less than.

A significant section of the act is those provisions involving the sale of marihuana to a minor by an adult. In addition to punishments based on the drug categories we see the criteria for imposing punishments becoming more concerned with the age of the minor. For example, if the minor who purchases marihuana or peyote from an adult is 18 to 20 years old, then the seller's punishment is two to six years imprisonment. However, if the minor is under 18, the seller's first offense is punishable by imprisonment of three to eight years and subsequent offenses are punishable by imprisonment of four to ten years. The criteria based on age do not cease here. If the seller is under 21, the punishment is then not more than five years.

A provision of the act further states that if a person is knowingly present where marihuana or peyote is kept or deposited or if a person is in the company of a person knowing that the other person is in possession of marihuana or peyote then he shall be imprisoned for not more than 11 months and be fined not more than $1,000.

The general penalty provisions of the statute directed at the amphetamines and barbiturates impose sentences much less severe than for those in other states. Offenses involving the amphetamines and barbiturates are punished by not more than six months imprisonment and/or a fine of $1,000.

Maryland: Md. Ann. Code Art. 27, Sec. 276 et seq.
(Supp. 1970)

Maryland, like Louisiana, has adopted a *Controlled Dangerous Substances Act* which is substantially similar to the *Federal Comprehensive Drug Abuse Prevention and Control Act of 1970.*

The Maryland act provides four schedules of drugs and the schedule under which a drug is classified depends upon whether it has a recognized medical use, whether it has a high potential for abuse and whether continued use of the drug will lead to severe physiological or psychological dependence.

Like the federal act, the law of Maryland permits a first offender to be placed on probation by the court providing he seeks in-patient or out-patient care pursuant to court orders. If the court orders are complied with for the stipulated period of time, then the accused will have his record expunged and he will have no public criminal record for purposes of employment, civil rights or any statute or regulation or license or questionnaire or any other public or private purpose.

This provision differs from the section in the federal act which provides that records may be expunged for first offenders because under the federal act only those under 21 may have their records expunged. In essence, the Maryland statute takes a more progressive approach in permitting a first offender to rehabilitate himself before he is imprisoned because the opportunity is given to all first offenders and not only to those who are under 21.

One more progressive measure in the Maryland statute is the section which provides that the unlawful possession of marihuana be considered a misdemeanor and punished by imprisonment of not more than one year and/or a fine of $1,000. Although marihuana is classified with the hallucinogenic substances in Schedule I, the legislature has apparently recognized the need to provide punishments which are less harsh. It is also significant to note that in classifying marihuana as an hallucinogenic substance the legislature has departed from traditionally categorizing marihuana as a narcotic. There are no provisions which *increase* the penalty for the sale of a controlled substance by an adult to a minor.

Massachusetts: Mass. Gen. Laws Ann. Ch. 94, Sec. 187 et seq. (Supp. 1970); Mass. Gen. Laws Ann. Ch. 94, Sec. 197 et seq. (Supp. 1970)

In highlighting provisions of Massachusetts laws relating to drug abuse, classification of drugs for purposes of imposing penalties becomes most significant. In most states the term "narcotic drug" refers to opiates and other drugs which are said to have a potential for addiction. In most other states the hallucinogenic drugs do not come within the definition of "narcotic drugs." This is basically because the hallucinogenic drugs, although having harmful effects, are generally not considered the type of drugs that lead to physical dependence.

TABLE XXIII—MARYLAND

Citation	Type of Drug	(Unlawful Manufacture, Unlawful Distribution, Possession with Intent to Distribute) General Penalty Provisions	Possession
Md. Ann. Code Article 27, Sec. 276 et seq. (Supp. 1970)	*Schedule I* (42 substances having no currently accepted medical use and having high potential for abuse; also 17 opium derivatives, including heroin, and 17 hallucinogens including mescaline, peyote and LSD)	*If Narcotic:* NMT 20 yrs. and NMT $25,000 *If Non-narcotic:* NMT 5 yrs. and/or $15,000 S: Twice the penalty of 1st	NMT 4 yrs. and/or a fine of NMT $25,000 *Except Marihuana* NMT 1 yr. and/or a fine of $1,000
	Schedule II A high potential for abuse and a currently accepted medical	*If Narcotic:* NMT 20 yrs. and NMT $25,000 *If Non-narcotic:*	Same as Above (Schedule I)

use in the United States: any narcotic substances not listed in other sections which are derived from opium, coca leaves and opiate & 20 enumerated opiates	NMT 5 yrs. and/or $15,000 S: Twice the penalty for 1st	
Schedule III Well documented medical use: Amphetamines and Barbiturates	NMT 5 yrs. and/or 15,000 S: Twice the penalty of 1st	Same as Above (Schedule I)
Schedule IV Accepted medical use and potential for abuse less than Schedule III	NMT 5 yrs. and/or $15,000 S: Twice the penalty of 1st	Same as Above (Schedule I)

1st = 1st offense.
2nd = 2nd offense.
3rd = 3rd offense.
S = Subsequent offense.
NMT = Not more than.
NLT = Not less than.

TABLE XXIV—MASSACHUSETTS

Citation	Type of Drug	General Penalty Provisions	Possession	Possession for Sale	Sale	Sale to Minor by Adult
Mass. Gen. Laws Ann. Ch. 94, Sec. 197 et seq. (Supp. 1970)	Narcotics: (including hallucinogens)	1st: NMT 2 yrs. and/or NMT $2,000 S: 5-10 yrs.	NMT 3½ yrs. in state prison or 2½ yrs. in jail and NMT $1,000	1st: 5-10 yrs. S: 10-25 yrs.	1st: 5-10 yrs. S: 10-25 yrs.	1st: 20-25 yrs. S: 20-50 yrs. (probation, suspension or parole prohibited after first offense).
	Heroin		1st: 2½ yrs. in jail or house of correction or NMT 5 yrs. in the state prison or NLT $500 nor more than $5,000 S: 5-15 yrs. in state prison	1st: 5-10 yrs. S: 10-25 yrs.	1st: 5-10 yrs. S: 10-25 yrs.	1st: 10-25 yrs. S: 20-50 yrs.
Ch. 94, Sec. 187 et seq.	Harmful Drugs (Amphetamines and Barbiturates)	NMT 2 yrs. or NMT $1,000	NMT 1 year or $500			

1st = 1st offense.
2nd = 2nd offense.

3rd = 3rd offense.
S = Subsequent offense.

NMT = Not more than.
NLT = Not less than.

In Massachusetts, however, the "narcotic drugs" include the hallucinogens. In defining "narcotic drugs" in the Uniform Narcotic Drug Law of Massachusetts the statute describes coca leaves (cocaine), morphine, heroin, codeine, peyote, LSD, psilocybin, dimethyltryptamine (DMT), marihuana (cannabis) and tetrahydrocannabinol (THC) and others. This definition of "narcotic drugs" which embraces not only the opiates and their derivatives but the hallucinogens and marihuana necessitates the imposition of harsh penalties for possession of these drugs.

The definition also reflects the response of the legislature to the abuse of synthetic substitutes for these drugs. "Narcotic drugs" includes the chemically synthetic substitutes for opium, morphine, heroin, cocaine and cannabis.

In contrast to some of the other states which have lessened the penalties for the possession of marihuana for personal use, Massachusetts has chosen to impose the general penalties which are invoked for offenses involving other narcotic drugs. Possession of narcotic drugs is punishable by imprisonment in the state prison of not more than three and one-half years or in the jail for not more than two and one-half years and a fine of not more than $1,000. This penalty is for possession of hallucinogens (LSD) or marihuana or the opiates except heroin. In an effort to deter the abuse of heroin, the legislature withdrew this narcotic drug from the general penalty provisions setting forth penalties for offenses involving narcotic drugs. Heroin is discussed in separate provisions which provide *specific* penalties for offenses involving this drug. The harsher penalties are an apparent effort to provide an increased deterrent for offenses involving this drug with a high potential for addiction. Therefore, the statute provides that possession of heroin is punishable by imprisonment of two and one-half years in a jail or house of correction or not more than five years in the state prison or a fine of not less than $500 nor more than $5,000. For a second or subsequent offense involving the possession of heroin the penalty is five to 15 years imprisonment in the state prison. The possession with intent to sell heroin or the sale of heroin is punishable by imprisonment of five to ten years for the first offense and 10 to 25 years for subsequent offenses. Similar penalties are provided for offenses involving the possession for sale or sale of other drugs defined as narcotic drugs.

The statute also prohibits the unauthorized sale or possession of a hypodermic syringe, hypodermic needle, or any instrument adopted for the administration of narcotic drugs by subcutaneous injection.

The unlawful possession of other harmful drugs (amphetamines and barbiturates) is punishable by imprisonment in a jail or house of correction for not more than one year or by a fine of not more than $500. The unauthorized sale, manufacture or importation of these drugs is also prohibited.

Michigan: Mich. Comp. Laws Ann. Sec. 335-51 et seq.
(Supp. 1970); Mich. Comp. Laws Ann. Sec. 335-106 et seq.
(Supp. 1970)

Michigan has adopted a traditional approach in classifying narcotics. In defining narcotic, the statute includes marihuana. This is the approach adopted by many states which have followed the definitions of the Uniform Narcotic Drug Act, in contrast to the approach adopted by the federal act which classifies marihuana as an hallucinogen along with LSD, DMT, peyote and mescaline. This should illustrate the importance of classification. In Michigan the possession of a substance defined as a "narcotic" is punishable by imprisonment of not more than 10 years while the possession of any hallucinogen is punishable as a felony. Since an accused's penalty is dependent on the type of drug involved in the selected offense, it should be objectively determined whether marihuana is an hallucinogen or a narcotic or the distinction for penalties should be removed.

The Michigan statute does not contain a provision for illegal sales of controlled drugs to minors. In addition, the laws of Michigan do not group the drugs in categories which take cognizance of whether a specific drug has an accepted medical use. This is one progressive approach in federal legislation and in the Louisiana and Maryland enactments which provide a more objective classification approach for purposes of imposing penalties. One provision of the Michigan Uniform Narcotic Drug

TABLE XXV—MICHIGAN

Citation	Type of Drug	General Penalty Provisions	Possession	Possession for Sale	Sale
Mich. Comp. Laws Ann. Sec. 335.51 et seq. (Supp. 1970)	Narcotics	Violations in sales by registrants: NMT 10 yrs. and/or a fine of NMT $10,000	1st: NMT 10 yrs. and a fine of NMT $5,000 2nd: NMT 20 yrs. and NMT $5,000 S: 20-40 yrs. and NMT $5,000	1st: NMT 10 yrs. and a fine of NMT $5,000 2nd: NMT 20 yrs. and NMT $5,000 S: 20-40 yrs. and NMT $5,000	20 yrs. to life
	Barbiturates		Misdemeanor: NMT 1 year and/or $5,000		Misdemeanor: NMT 1 year and/or $5,000
Mich. Comp. Laws Ann. Sec. 335.106 (Supp. 1970)	Hallucinogens (LSD, DMT, Peyote, Mescaline)		NMT 4 years	NMT 4 years	NMT 4 years

1st = 1st offense.
2nd = 2nd offense.
3rd = 3rd offense.
S = Subsequent offense.

NMT = Not more than.
NLT = Not less than.

Act states that information communicated to a physician in an effort unlawfully to procure a narcotic drug or unlawfully to procure the administration of such drug shall not be deemed a privileged communication. Essentially, this makes the task of prosecuting an offender less difficult because ordinarily any statement made by a patient to a physician is inadmissible at the trial of a defendant.

Minnesota: Minn. Stat. Ann., Sec. 618 et seq. (1963);
Minn. Stat. Ann., Sec. 152 et seq. (1963)

Minnesota has not enacted any substantial legislation relating to narcotics since 1963. The laws relating to other regulated drugs do not reflect the recent legislative concern over classification as many other states have indicated. The Minnesota statute approaches the problem of drug abuse by providing very general penalty provisions. It is apparent that the discretion involved in imposing sentence is placed more upon the court than upon the legislature. This is illustrated by the general penalty provisions which state that a violation of the Minnesota Uniform Narcotic Drug Act involves a sentence of five to 20 years and a fine of not more than $20,000. This penalty is imposed in all *narcotic* related offenses except in offense involving the sale of a narcotic drug to a minor where the penalty is 10 to 40 years in prison and a fine of $20,000. This should illustrate that there is a maximum of discretion vested in the court to decide what type of sentence will be imposed for the varied types of narcotic related offenses. This may be contrasted to the laws of most other states which *statutorily* provide sentences for the different narcotic related offenses. For example, the New York law relating to narcotics provides a scheme of sentences based not only on the type of offenses but also based upon the amount of the specific narcotic involved.

In Minnesota the court merely works within the framework of the statutory guidelines setting forth a general penalty provision of five to 20 years and a fine of not more than $10,000. This means that the court may view the nature of the offense (e.g., sale or possession, etc.) and then impose sentence based upon the severity of the offense. However, this often leads to harsh

TABLE XXVI—MINNESOTA

Citation	Type of Drug	General Penalty Provisions	Sale to Minor by Adult
Minn. Stat. Ann., Sec. 618 et seq. (1963)	Narcotics	NMT $10,000 and 5-20 years	$20,000 fine and 10-40 years
Minn. Stat. Ann., Sec. 152 et seq. (1963)	Stimulants and Depressants (Amphetamines, Barbiturates, LSD, DMT, Mescaline)	NMT 1 yr.	

1st = 1st offense.
2nd = 2nd offense.
3rd = 3rd offense.
S = Subsequent offense.

NMT = Not more than.
NLT = Not less than.

sentences. In the case of *Steeves v. State* (178 N.W.2d 723) the defendant was found with a pink pill known commercially as Percodan-Demi® in his possession. This pill is a chemical preparation of an alkaloid of the narcotic drug opium. The trial court imposed a ten year sentence upon Steeves pursuant to the general penalty provision which states possession of a narcotic drug is punishable by a sentence of five to 20 years and a fine of not more than $10,000. This penalty was imposed upon the defendant despite the fact that he was a first offender. The defendant appealed the sentence stating it was cruel and unusual punishment to impose a ten year sentence upon him for possessing a pink pill which was a chemical preparation derived from opium. The Supreme Court of Minnesota affirmed the sentence stating that the defendant's sentence of ten years imprisonment for possession of narcotics under the statute providing for penalties of not less than five nor more than 20 years imprisonment was not cruel and unusual punishment although he was a first offender and was in possession of only a small amount of narcotics.

Marihuana is classified as a narcotic drug and therefore harsh penalties may be imposed for offenses involving this drug.

A separate chapter, entitled *Prohibited Drugs,* regulates the sale and possession of the stimulant, depressant and hallucinogenic drugs. The most significant section of this chapter is the section defining "Depressant or Stimulant Drug." A depressant or stimulant drug includes the amphetamines, barbiturates, LSD, DMT (dimethyltryptamine), "or any drug which contains a quantity of a substance designated by regulations promulgated by the board of pharmacy as having shown a potential for abuse and injurious to health because of its *depressant or stimulant effect* on the central nervous system *or its hallucinogenic effect.*" This indicates that Minnesota has grouped the stimulants, depressants and hallucinogens together for purposes of imposing penalties for violations involving these drugs. This is in sharp contrast to the federal statute and most state laws which separate the hallucinogens from the stimulants and depressants because of the hallucinogens' greater potential for abuse. However, it is also interesting to note that all offenses involving these drugs are treated as a misdemeanor and punishable by not more than one year in jail and/or a fine of not more than $1,000. This is in sharp contrast to the harsher penalties invoked in most other states for offenses involving the possession or sale of hallucinogens.

Mississippi: Miss. Code Ann., Sec. 6831-52 et seq. (Supp. 1971)

Mississippi, along with Louisiana and Maryland, has enacted a Uniform Controlled Substances Act which is substantially similar to the *Federal Drug Abuse Prevention and Control Act of 1970.* The Mississippi statute, like the federal statute, classifies the drugs into five schedules, and penalties are imposed for the unlawful manufacture, delivery or possession of these controlled substances. The penalties imposed are based on the schedule under which the drug is classified. In addition, if a drug is a narcotic drug (heroin) as contrasted to a non-narcotic drug (marihuana, mescaline or peyote), the offense involves a greater punishment despite the fact that the substances are both classified in Schedule I.

The Mississippi Bureau of Drug Enforcement, under the supervision and control of the Mississippi State Board of Health, is clothed with the authority of classifying the drugs within the respective schedules. The statute provides that in making a determination regarding a substance the Board is to consider:

(1) The actual or relative potential for abuse;
(2) the scientific evidence of its pharmacological effect, if known;
(3) the state of current scientific knowledge regarding the substance;
(4) the history and current pattern of abuse;
(5) the scope, duration and significance of abuse;
(6) the risk of public health;
(7) the potential of the substance to produce psychic or physiological dependence liability; and
(8) whether the substance is an immediate percursor of a substance already controlled.

TABLE XXVII—MISSISSIPPI

Citation	Type of Drug	General Penalty Provisions	Sale to Minor by Adult	Other Offenses
Uniform Controlled Substances Act Miss. Code Ann. Sec. 6831-52 et seq. (Supp. 1971)	Schedule I: 42 opiates, 22 opium derivatives (including heroin) and 17 hallucinogenic substances (LSD, Marihuana, mescaline, and peyote)	Possess, deliver or manufacture if: Narcotic in Schedule I: 1st: NMT 6 yrs. and/or $2,000 S: Twice penalty of 1st. Non-narcotic in Schedule I: 1st: NMT 4 yrs. and/or $2,000 S: Twice penalty of 1st	Narcotic: 1st: NMT 2 yrs. and/or $2,000 S: Double Penalty imprisonment, same fine	Unlawful dispensation of a controlled substance by a registrant: NMT 1 yr. and/or NMT $1,000
	Schedule II: Any opium derivatives not listed in Schedule I, and coca leaves and 21 specific opiates including methadone	Narcotic: 1st: NMT 6 yrs. and/or $2,000 S: twice 1st Non-narcotic: 1st: NMT 4 yrs. and/or $2,000 S: twice 1st	Double penalty, imprisonment—same fine	

Schedule III: (Amphetamine or Barbiturates)	1st: NMT 4 yrs. and/or $2,000 S: twice 1st	Double penalty, imprisonment—same fine
Schedule IV: 11 specific substances with a depressant effect on the central nervous system	1st: NMT 2 yrs. and/or $1,000 S: twice 1st	Double penalty, imprisonment—same fine
Schedule V: compounds containing the following narcotic drugs, also containing 1 or more non-narcotic active medical ingredients	1st: NMT 6 mos. and/or $500 S: twice 1st	Double penalty, imprisonment—same fine

1st = 1st offense.
2nd = 2nd offense.

3rd = 3rd offense.
S = Subsequent offense.

NMT = Not more than.
NLT = Not less than.

The Mississippi act does not include the progressive provisions contained in the federal act relating to the dismissal of charges against first offenders and no provision is contained in the act relating to the suspension of sentence and the expungement of records whereby possession offenses are dismissed if probationary requirements are complied with under the federal drug law.

Missouri: Mo. Rev. Stat., Sec. 195 et seq. (Supp. 1970)

Missouri has not departed from the traditional classification of dangerous drugs. The laws relating to drug abuse are directed at two major categories of drugs. These classifications are narcotic drugs and the stimulants, depressants and hallucinogens. Harsher penalties are imposed in Missouri for narcotic related offenses than in most other states; however, a large degree of sentencing discretion does exist as indicated by the statute which provides that the unlawful manufacture, delivery or possession of a narcotic drug is punishable by not more than 20 years in prison, or six months to one year in city jail. A subsequent offense is punishable by 10 years to life. However, a first offense involving the sale of a narcotic is punishable by five years to life. *A sale to a minor of a narcotic drug is statutorily punishable by death.* Marihuana is classified as a narcotic drug for purposes of imposing penalties.

A separate part of the act imposes lesser penalties for the unlawful manufacture, delivery or possession of "barbiturates," "hallucinogenic drugs" or "stimulant" drugs.

A "barbiturate" is defined as the salts and derivatives of barbituric acid or compounds, preparations, or mixtures thereof which have a hypnotic or somnifacient effect on the central nervous system of a human or animal.

An "hallucinogenic" drug is defined as meaning and including "mescaline or peyote, lysergic acid diethylamide, and psilocybin and any salts, isomers or combinations of salts and isomers thereof which have a depressant or stimulating effect on the central nervous system or an hallucinogenic effect."

"Stimulant" is defined as "amphetamine or any of its derivatives which have an exciting effect on the central nervous system of a human or animal."

TABLE XXVIII–MISSOURI

Citation	Type of Drug	General Penalty Provisions	Sale	Sale to Minor by Adult
Mo. Rev. Stat. Sec. 195 et seq. (Supp. 1970)	Narcotic	1st: NMT 20 years in prison or 6 months to one year in city jail 2nd: 5 yrs. to life S: 10 yrs. to life	1st: 5 yrs. to life S: 10 yrs. to life	Death
	Amphetamines, Barbiturates, Hallucinogenics	Prison: 2-10 years or city jail NMT 1 yr. and/or NMT $1,000		

1st = 1st offense.
2nd = 2nd offense.

3rd = 3rd offense.
S   = Subsequent offense.

NMT = Not more than.
NLT = Not less than.

The Division of Health of the Missouri Department of Health and Welfare prepares a list of all the drugs falling within the purview of the terms barbiturate, stimulant or hallucinogenic drug. After preparation a copy of the list is filed in the Office of the Secretary of State. It is apparent that these definitions are arbitrary and overlap to some degree. However, it is significant to consider whether any of the drugs which are presently classified as narcotics come within the purview of the definitions promulgated for "barbiturates," "stimulants" or "hallucinogenic substances." This gathers particular importance when we consider the disparity in sentences which are imposed for offenses involving these dangerous substances based on the consideration of whether they are classified as narcotic or stimulating barbiturate or hallucinogenic drugs.

Montana: Mont. Rev. Codes Ann., Sec. 54-129 et seq.
(Supp. 1970)

Montana has recently amended the laws regulating dangerous drugs. These amendments, embraced in the Montana Dangerous Drug Act, do not emphasize the classification of drugs for purposes of imposing penalties. "Dangerous drugs" are defined in the act as any depressant, stimulant, hallucinogenic or narcotic drug. The act then provides penalties for the unlawful manufacture, sale or possession of any of the dangerous drugs. Therefore there is no statutory distinction for purposes of imposing a penalty, which considers the type of dangerous drug which is unlawfully manufactured, possessed or sold. The penalty imposed is the same whether the substance involved is a depressant drug such as phenobarbital or an hallucinogenic drug such as lysergic acid diethylamide. Ostensibly, the legislature has found it more expedient to punish the substantive criminal act rather than imposing sentences based on sophisticated classifications. Although the legislature has not taken cognizance of the drug categories utilized by many other states for purposes of imposing penalties, definitions of the dangerous drugs are contained in the statute. Since "dangerous drugs" are defined as any "depressant, stimulant, hallucinogenic or narcotic drug" it became necessary to define those types of drugs. *Depressant drugs,* within this act,

TABLE XXIX—MONTANA

Citation	Possession	Sale and Similar Transaction	Other Offenses
Mont. Rev. Codes Ann. Sec. 54-129 et seq. (Supp. 1970)	All Dangerous Drugs (Except Marihuana): NMT 5 years 60 grams or less of Marihuana or 1 gram or less of hashish: NMT 1 yr. and/or $1,000 If defendant is a first offender and is 21 or less, he is entitled to a deferred imposition of sentence.	One year-life. If defendant is a first offender and 21 or less, he is entitled to a deferred imposition of sentence.	Fraudulently obtaining dangerous drugs: (not more than six months).

1st = 1st offense.
2nd = 2nd offense.

3rd = 3rd offense.
S   = Subsequent offense.

NMT = Not more than.
NLT = Not less than.

include amobarbital, secobarbital, pentobarbital, phenobarbital, barbituric acid, glutethimide, meprobamate, chloral hydrate, paraldehyde, ethclorvynol, and ethinamate or any product, derivative, compound or preparation containing the above listed drugs.

The *stimulant drugs* include amphetamine, dextroamphetamine, mephentermine, methamphetamine and phenmetrazine, or any product, compound or derivative of the above listed drugs.

The *hallucinogenic drugs* include marihuana, lysergic acid diethylamide, psilocybin, dimethyltryptamine, methyltryptamine, peyote and mescaline or any product, derivative, compound or preparation of the above listed drugs. It is significant to note that under the previous Montana drug law, marihuana was legally defined as a narcotic. The present classification of marihuana as an hallucinogenic substance is similar to the classification under the *Federal Drug Abuse Prevention and Control Act of 1970* which groups marihuana with the hallucinogenic substances.

The Montana act includes opium, morphine, heroin, codeine ethylmorphine, dihydromorphinone, Isonipecaine, methadone and cocaine and compounds and derivatives of these drugs within the "narcotic drug" definition.

However, as mentioned above, since these classifications become superfluous for purposes of imposing penalties for offenses involving these drugs, the criteria used for purposes of classification is of little importance.

Possession of all dangerous drugs is punishable by imprisonment of not more than five years. A statutory exception is provided where the offense is possession of 60 grams or less of marihuana or one gram or less of hashish. In these instances, the possession is punishable by not more than one year in prison and/or a $1,000 fine.

The unlawful manufacture or sale of any dangerous drug is punishable by one year to life imprisonment.

A provision in the statute provides that if the defendant is a first offender and 21 years or less, he is entitled to a deferred imposition of sentence.

The case of *State v. Dunn* (472 P.2d 288, 1970) reflects the advantages of not tailoring the penalties to the type of drug involved. In this case, the Supreme Court of Montana *held* that a conviction was proper despite the fact that the pills in question had been ingested by recipients and were consequently unavailable for precise chemical analysis. The described hallucinations by the recipients and the testimony of the attending physician, without a definite description of the dangerous drug involved, was sufficient to sustain the defendant's conviction for criminal sale of dangerous drugs. In this case, the sentencing court would have encountered some obstacles if the sentence to be imposed depended upon the type of dangerous drug involved.

Nebraska: 28-451 et seq. (Supp. 1969); 28-485 et seq. (Supp. 1969)

Nebraska recognizes three basic categories for purposes of imposing penalties for drug related offenses. These categories are narcotics, marihuana or delta and delta-transhydrocannabinol, and depressant, stimulant or hallucinogenic drugs. The legislature has apparently chosen to impose different penalties for offenses involving these varied categories of drugs. The penalties imposed for offenses involving the narcotic drugs and the depressant, stimulant, or hallucinogenic drugs are similar to the provisions of many other states. However, the penalties imposed for possession of marihuana and delta-transhydrocannabinol are somewhat unique. Even this category is sub-divided into two categories for purposes of imposing penalties. The possession of small amounts of marihuana involves a penalty of seven days in the county jail for a first offense. A subsequent offense is punishable by one to five years in prison. The seven-day sentence is much less severe than that imposed in other jurisdictions. However, the possession of tetrahydrocannabinol (THC) is punishable by three to six months in the county jail and a $300 to $500 fine.

The separate provisions promulgating the penalties for possession of marihuana and THC are somewhat paradoxical in view of the fact that Nebraska defines "narcotic drugs" as meaning coca leaves, opium, cannabis, Isonipecaine, Amidone, isoami-

TABLE XXX—NEBRASKA

Citation	Type of Drug	General Penalty Provisions	Possession	Possession for Sale	Sale and Similar Transaction
Narcotic Drugs: 28-451 et seq. (1969 Supp.)	Narcotic	1st: 2-5 yrs. and NMT $3,000 2nd: 5-10 yrs. and NMT $5,000 S: 10-20 yrs. and NMT $5,000			
	Marihuana and delta-transhydrocannabinol and tetra-hydro-cannabinol (THC)		Marihuana: 1st: 7 days in county jail S: 1-5 yrs. THC: 1st: 3-6 mos. or $300-$500 fine S: 1-5 yrs.	Possession for sale presumed where possession is of (a) 25 or more cigarettes containing cannabis or (b) ½ pound or more: 1-5 yrs.	1st and S: 2-5 yrs.
Sec. 28-485 et seq. (Supp. 1969)	Depressant and stimulant drugs (Barbiturates, Amphetamines and Hallucinogens)	1st: 2-5 yrs. and/or $500-$3,000 fine S: 5-10 yrs. and/or $1,000-$5,000 fine			

1st = 1st offense.   3rd   = 3rd offense.   NMT = Not more than.
2nd = 2nd offense.   S   = Subsequent offense.   NLT = Not less than.

done and ketobemidone. Since the penalties for possession of marihuana are less than those for offenses involving all other narcotic drugs one would expect the legislature to exclude marihuana from the list of narcotic drugs.

Nevada: Nev. Rev. Stat. Ch. 453 and Ch. 454 (1967)

Nevada classifies drugs as either narcotic, dangerous, or hallucinogenic. The narcotic drugs include coca leaves, opium, Isonipecaine, cannabis and every other substance neither chemically nor physically distinguishable from them and any other drugs to which the federal laws relating to narcotics may now apply. The Uniform Narotic Drug Act of Nevada classifies marihuana as a narcotic.

Offenses involving hallucinogenic drugs carry less stringent penalties and it therefore becomes important to determine whether Nevada's classifications are scientifically objective.

The second category of controlled substances is *dangerous drugs.* These are defined as any substance:

1. "Which the director of the Bureau of Narcotics and Dangerous Drugs of the United States Department of Justice, after investigation, has found to have and by regulation designates as having, a potential for abuse because of its depressant or stimulant effect on the central nervous system *or its hallucinogenic effect";*

2. "any drug which has been approved by the Food and Drug Administration for general distribution and bears the legend: 'Caution: Federal Law prohibits dispensing without prescription,' or"

3. "drug sales which have been restricted to prescription by regulation adopted by the state authorities, because the State Board of Health finds these drugs dangerous to public health or safety."

There are provisions which are specifically directed at regulating the refill of prescriptions for dangerous drugs. The prescriptions for these drugs are not to be refilled more than five times or for more than a period of six months, whichever occurs first. These laws seem to be directed at controlling drugs such as amphetamines and barbiturates which have a currently accepted

TABLE XXXI—NEVADA

Citation	Type of Drug	General Penalty Provisions	Possession	Sale and Similar Transactions	Sale to Minor by Adult	Other Offenses
Nev. Rev. Stat. Ch. 453 and Ch. 454 (1967)	Narcotics (including Marihuana) (Ch. 453)	1st: 1-6 yrs. and NMT $2,000 2nd: 1-10 yrs. and NMT $2,000 S: 1-20 yrs. and NMT $5,000		1st: 1-20 yrs. and NMT $5,000 S: Life (no parole) and NMT $5,000	1st: Life (parole possible after 7 yrs.) and NMT $5,000 S: Life—no parole	*Trafficking* 1st: Life (parole after 7 yrs.) and NMT $5,000 2nd: Life—no parole *Planting Marihuana* 1st: 1-6 yrs. and fine of NMT $2,000 2nd: 1-10 yrs. and a fine of NMT $2,000
Ch. 454 (454.180 et seq.)	Dangerous Drugs		1st and 2nd: Gross misdemeanor S: 1-10 yrs.	1st and 2nd: Gross misdemeanor S: 1-10 yrs.	1-10 yrs. and NMT $5,000	
	Hallucinogenic Drugs	1st: 1-6 yrs. and NMT $2,000 2nd: 1-10 yrs. and NMT $2,000 S: 1-20 yrs. and NMT $5,000		1st: 1-20 yrs. and NMT $5,000 (parole eligibility after 7 yrs.) S: Life—no parole eligibility	1st: Life (possibility of probation) S: Life (no probation possibility)	

1st = 1st offense.
2nd = 2nd offense.
3rd = 3rd offense.
S = Subsequent offense.
NMT = Not more than.
NLT = Not less than.

medical use. Although the classification based on the presence or lack of a currently accepted medical use as followed in the federal law is not expressly stated in the Nevada law, it is apparent that this was a tacit consideration. This is illustrated by the separate provisions relating to hallucinogenic drugs. This section specifically refers to lysergic acid, d-lysergic acid diethylamide (LSD) and N-N-dimethyltryptamine. Although the dangerous drugs section includes drugs having an hallucinogenic effect, by specifically listing some hallucinogenic drugs, the legislature imposes harsher penalties for offenses involving these substances.

It is significant to note that the penalties provided for offenses involving hallucinogenic drugs are similar to those provided for narcotic drugs even though the drugs are separately classified.

New Hampshire: N.H. Laws 318-B:1 et seq. (Supp. 1970)

The Controlled Drug Act of New Hampshire provides that "controlled drugs are those drugs and chemicals which contain any quantity of a substance which has been designated as subject to federal narcotic laws, or which has been designated as a depressant or stimulant drug pursuant to federal food and drug laws, or which has been by regulation, after investigation and hearing designated by the Division of Public Health Services as 'having a stimulant, depressant or hallucinogenic effect upon the higher functions of the central nervous system and as having a potential for abuse or physiological and psychological dependence, or both.' " The statute states that controlled drugs are classifiable as amphetamine-type, barbiturate-type, cannabis-type, cocaine-type, hallucinogenic, morphine-type and other stimulant and depressant drugs. Although the statute does not list specific drugs under any of these categories, the classifications are superfluous because the penalties imposed are based solely on the consideration of whether the controlled substance is a narcotic. For example, the sale of a narcotic drug is punishable by not more than 20 years and/or not more than $5,000 for a first offense, but the sale of *any* other controlled substance is punishable by not more than 10 years and/or not more than $2,000. Consequently, it is unimportant whether a drug involved in a sale is an hallucinogenic drug or a stimulant-type drug, because

TABLE XXXII—NEW HAMPSHIRE

Citation	Type of Drug	Possession	Sale and Similar Transactions
N. H. Laws 318-B: 1 et seq. (Supp. 1970)	Narcotic (not including marihuana)	1st: NMT 5 years and/or NMT $2,000 S: NMT 10 years and/or $5,000	1st: NMT 20 years and/or NMT $5,000 S: NMT 25 years
	Any controlled drug other than narcotic	1st: NMT one year and/or NMT $500 S: NMT 3 years and/or NMT $1,000 One pound or more of any cannabis-type drug: 1st: NMT 5 yrs. and/or NMT $2,000 S: NMT 10 years and/or $5,000	1st: NMT 10 years and/or NMT $2,000 S: NMT 15 years and/or NMT $5,000

1st = 1st offense.
2nd = 2nd offense.
3rd = 3rd offense.
S = Subsequent offense.
NMT = Not more than.
NLT = Not less than.

the main categories are merely narcotic and non-narcotic for purposes of imposing penalties. This is in contrast to some states where different penalties are imposed for offenses involving varied types of non-narcotic substances. For example, many states punish the sale of hallucinogenic substances more severely than the sale of other dangerous types of drugs, such as amphetamines and barbiturates.

Although New Hampshire only considers whether the drug is a narcotic or non-narcotic for purposes of imposing penalties, the statute contains some excellent definitions of substances which are controlled. For example, hallucinogenic drugs are statutorily defined as "psychodysleptic drugs which assert a confusional or disorganized effect upon mental processes or behavior and mimic acute psychotic disturbances. Exemplary of such drugs are mescaline, peyote, psilocybin and d-lysergic acid diethylamine." The statute also defines cocaine-type drugs, cannabis-type drugs, barbiturate-type drugs, and amphetamine-type drugs. These definitive guidelines may prevent confusion when a drug is classified. It will further aid in preventing a drug which is a stimulant or depressant type of drug from being classified as an hallucinogenic drug. Many states which provide for categorizing a drug as an hallucinogenic or stimulant or depressant type of substance do not provide sufficient and informative definitions of these substances.

New Jersey: N.J. Rev. Stat., Sec. 24:21-1 et seq.
(Supp. 1971)

The New Jersey Controlled Dangerous Substances Act is similar to the classification approach promulgated by the federal government in the *Federal Drug Abuse Prevention and Control Act of 1970.*

The New Jersey act has classified the controlled substances within four schedules contrasted to the five schedules used to categorize dangerous substances under the federal act. New Jersey has combined the barbiturates and amphetamines within one schedule contrasted to the federal act which classifies amphetamines under Schedule III and barbiturates under Schedule IV.

The New Jersey statute provides the same criteria as the fed-

TABLE XXXIII—NEW JERSEY

Citation	Type of Drug	Possession	Manufacture, Sale and Similar Transaction	Sale to Minor by Adult	Other Offenses
N. J. Rev. Stat. Sec. 24:21-1 et seq. (Supp. 1971)	*Schedule I:* 42 opiates, 23 narcotic substances (including heroin) 17 hallucinogenic substances (including marihuana, mescaline, peyote and tetrahydrocannabinols).	Any controlled substance within Schedule I, NMT 5 yrs. and/or $15,000, but if possession is 25 grams or less of marihuana or 5 grams or less of hashish, then punished pursuant to penalty imposed for disorderly persons which is NMT 6 mos. and/or a $500 fine	Narcotic drug within Schedule I: NMT 12 yrs. and/or NMT $25,000 Non-narcotic controlled substance: NMT 5 yrs. and/or NMT $15,000 S: NMT twice above penalty	NMT twice the penalty imposed for ordinary sale	Registration violations, NMT 3 yrs. and/or $30,000 Being under the influence of any controlled substance in Schedules I-IV: Disorderly person— punishable by NMT 6 mos. and/or $500 and loss of driving privileges
	Schedule II: Opium and opiate and any derivative or compound; coca leaves and 21 specifically enumerated opiates.	Any controlled substance within Schedule II, NMT 5 yrs. and/or $15,000 S: NMT twice above penalty	Narcotic drug within Schedule II: NMT 12 yrs. and/or $25,000 Non-narcotic controlled substance, NMT 5 yrs. and/or NMT $15,000 S: NMT twice above penalty	NMT twice the penalty imposed for ordinary sale	Registration violations, NMT 3 yrs. and/or $30,000

Schedule III: Substances with stimulating effect on central nervous system (amphetamine). Substances with depressant effect on central nervous system (barbiturates) and compounds containing limited quantities of narcotic ingredients

Any controlled substance within Schedule III, NMT 5 yrs. and/or $15,000
S: NMT twice above penalty

1st: NMT 5 yrs. and/or NMT $15,000
S: NMT twice above penalty

NMT twice the penalty imposed for ordinary sale

Registration violations, NMT 3 yrs. and/or $30,000

Schedule IV: same as above

NMT 1 year and/or NMT $5,000

NMT 1 year and/or NMT $5,000

NMT twice the penalty for ordinary sale

1st = 1st offense.
2nd = 2nd offense.

3rd = 3rd offense.
S = Subsequent offense.

NMT = Not more than.
NLT = Not less than.

eral act does for classifying a controlled substance. A substance is scheduled based on the degree of current medical use if any, its potential for abuse relative to other controlled substances, and the degree of physiological or psychological dependence the use of the drug may lead to.

Marihuana is classified within Schedule I, which provides for drugs which have no currently accepted medical use. It is grouped with the hallucinogenic substances such as psilocybin, mescaline, peyote and LSD. However, the penalties imposed for possession of marihuana varies to some extent from the penalties incurred for possession of the other hallucinogenic drugs. Possession of the hallucinogenic drugs such as peyote, mescaline, or LSD is punishable by imprisonment of not more than five years and/or a fine of $15,000. Although marihuana is grouped with these hallucinogenic substances in Schedule I a less severe punishment is provided for possession of this controlled substance. Possession of 25 grams or less of marihuana or five grams or less of hashish renders the offender a disorderly person. Being adjudged a disorderly person in New Jersey is punishable by imprisonment of not more than six months and/or a fine of $500. In addition the right to operate a motor vehicle may be revoked for a period of not more than two years. The New Jersey act also provides that any person under the influence of any controlled substance may be adjudged a disorderly person and punished by imprisonment of not more than six months and/or $500.

The statute also provides that any person who is at least 18 years of age who distributes a controlled substance to a person 17 years of age or younger who is at least three years his junior is punishable by a term of imprisonment of up to twice that authorized for a sale made by an adult to an adult.

The statute contains progressive provisions which give the court discretion in conditionally discharging first offenders. Under these circumstances the accused pleads guilty or is found guilty but a judgment of conviction is postponed and the defendant is placed on probation. If the accused fulfills the terms and conditions of probation, the court discharges the accused and the proceedings are dismissed. A discharge and dismissal under this section is without court adjudication of guilt and is not deemed a conviction for purposes of disqualifications or disabilities. Discharge and dismissal under this section may occur only once with respect to any person. Upon violation of a term or condition of probation, the court may enter an adjudication of guilt and proceed as otherwise provided.

If a person is 21 years of age or younger at the time of his conviction, six months after the expiration of the term of probation he may apply to the court to have all records of his arrest, trial and conviction expunged. The effect of such a provision is to restore such person in the contemplation of the law to the status he occupied prior to such arrest and trial. In essence, this provision prevents young offenders of drug abuse laws from incurring disabilities as a consequence of having acquired a criminal record.

New Mexico: N.M. Stat. Ann. 54-6-51 et seq. (Supp. 1971)

New Mexico has three separate acts regulating the manufacture, sale or possession of substances which have demonstrated a potential for abuse. The first provision is part of the *Drug and Cosmetics Act,* which sets forth penalties for the unlawful manufacture, sale or possession of dangerous drugs. The dangerous drugs within contemplation of this act are stimulants, depressants and hallucinogens. In providing penalties for violations of the prohibited acts relating to these drugs, it is significant to note that DMT and LSD have been dealt with exclusively in this statute. Therefore, although these drugs are grouped with the amphetamines, barbiturates and hallucinogens harsher penalties are provided for the unlawful possession or sale of LSD or DMT than for the other drugs with which they are grouped. For example, a first offense involving possession of any stimulant, depressant or hallucinogenic drug is a misdemeanor and is punishable by imprisonment of not more than one year and/or a fine of not more than $1,000. However, if the unlawful possession is of LSD or DMT the first offense is a fourth degree felony and is punishable by imprisonment of one to five

TABLE XXXIV—NEW MEXICO

Citation	Type of Drug	Possession	Possession With Intent to Sell, Sale and Similar Transactions	Sale to Minor
N. M. Stat. Ann. 54-6-51 et seq. (Supp. 1971)	Narcotic Drugs: (marihuana not included) N.M. Stat. Ann. 54-7-1 et seq. (Supp. 1971)	1st: 4th Degree felony, 1-5 yrs. and/or $5,000 2nd: 3rd Degree felony, 2-10 yrs. and/or $5,000 S: 2nd Degree felony, 10-50 yrs. and/or $50,000	1st: 2nd Degree felony, 10-50 yrs. and/or $50,000 S: 1st Degree felony, life imprisonment and/or $15,000 fine	
	Marihuana Act N. M. Stat. Ann. 54-9-1 et seq. (Supp. 1971) including marihuana, hashish and tetrahydrocannabinols (THC)	One ounce or less of marihuana: 1st: petty misdemeanor, NMT 6 mos. and/or $100 S: 4th Degree felony 1-5 yrs. and/or $5,000 More than one ounce of marihuana or any amount of hashish or THC: 1st: 4th Degree felony	Marihuana, THC, or Hashish: 1st: 3rd Degree felony, 2-10 yrs. and/or $5,000 2nd: 2nd Degree felony, 10-50 yrs. and/or $10,000 S: 1st Degree felony, life imprisonment and/or $15,000	

Stimulant, depressant and Hallucinogenic Drugs (Marihuana excluded) N. M. Stat. Ann. 54-6-51 et seq. (Supp. 1971)	1-5 yrs. and/or $5,000 S: 3rd Degree felony 2-10 yrs. and/or $5,000 1st: NMT 1 yr. and/or $1,000 S: NMT 3 yrs. and/or $3,000 Separate provisions relating to the possession of LSD or DMT (Dimethytryptamine) 1st: 4th Degree felony, 1-5 yrs., and/or $5,000 2nd: 3rd Degree felony, 2-10 yrs. and/or $5,000	1st: 4th Degree felony 1-5 yrs. and/or $5,000 S: 3rd Degree felony 2-10 yrs. and/or $5,000 Separate provisions relating to the sale of LSD or DMT 1st: 3rd Degree felony 2-10 years and/or $5,000	1st: 3rd Degree felony 2-10 years and/or $5,000 S: 2nd Degree felony 10-50 years and/or $50,000

1st = 1st offense.
2nd = 2nd offense.

3rd = 3rd offense.
S = Subsequent offense.

NMT = Not more than.
NLT = Not less than.

years and/or a fine of $3,000. Ostensibly, the statute attempts to provide a deterrent effect for offenses involving these drugs because of their greater potential for abuse and the possibility of greater harmful effects.

New Mexico also has a *Narcotic Drug Act* which prohibits the unlawful manufacture, sale or possession of narcotics. The amended Narcotic Drug Act has omitted marihuana from the definition of narcotics. Under the 1971 Act, narcotic drugs are defined as "opium, isonipecaine, coca leaves (cocaine), opiate, methadone, phenazocine, and levorphanol." Marihuana, hashish and tetrahydrocannabinol are treated exclusively in the New Mexico Marihuana Act. Since marihuana is no longer classified with the narcotic substances in New Mexico as it was prior to enacting the new law, the unlawful manufacture, sale or possession of this substance is punished separate from other laws relating to drug abuse. The effect of such a separate act is that it now provides penalties less harsh than for offenses involving narcotic drugs. The first offense involving possession of one ounce or less of marihuana is now a petty misdemeanor which is punishable by imprisonment of not more than six months and/or a fine of $100. It is noteworthy that hashish and tetrahydrocannabinol are included in the definition of marihuana but a first offense involving these dangerous substances is punishable as a fourth degree felony and involves a sentence of one to five years and/or a fine of $5,000.

The New Mexico Marihuana Act of 1971 provides that a first offender may have the charges dismissed if he complies with the conditions of probation. In addition if the offender is 21 years of less, then the criminal record including the arrest, trial, and conviction may be expunged. This is similar to the federal provisions and to the provisions of New Jersey. However, the dismissal privilege and rights to have the records expunged in New Mexico only prevail where the offense involves cannabis, hashish, or tetrahydrocannabinols (THC). This is in contrast to the similar dismissal privileges and rights to have the records expunged in federal cases and in New Jersey in offenses involving all types of controlled substances.

New York: N.Y. Penal Law, Sec. 220 et seq. (Supp. 1970)

New York punishes two types of offenses involving dangerous drugs: possession and sale.

Possession offenses may occur in one of six degrees. Selling offenses may occur in one of four degrees. The degree of the offenses is based not only on the type of drug involved but also on the quantity. New York places particular emphasis on the amount of the dangerous drug which is involved in the described offense.

Section 3301 of the Public Health Law of New York includes marihuana in its definition of narcotic drugs. However, possession of dangerous drugs in the first and second degree does not include marihuana although the possession must be of a narcotic drug. The legislature chose to exclude marihuana from these harsh punishment offenses despite the fact that marihuana is still defined as a "narcotic." A similar criticism exists when analyzing the section relating to the sale of "narcotic drugs." One may also question the wisdom of providing less severe punishment for offenses involving the depressants, stimulants and hallucinogens in view of the fact that these drugs are the substances which are most increasingly abused. The hallucinogenic substances include mescaline, peyote, lysergic acid diethylamide (LSD) and psilocybin.

North Carolina: N.C. Gen. Stat. 90-86 et seq. (Supp. 1969)

North Carolina *broadly* defines narcotics. Narcotics include most of the drugs which have demonstrated a potential for abuse except the stimulant and depressant drugs. The statute provides that narcotic drugs mean coca leaves (cocaine), opium, opium poppy, cannabidial, tetrahydrocannabinol, cannabis, peyote, mescaline, psilocybe, mexicana, *psilocybin, lysergic acid diethylamide (LSD) or other psychedelic drugs or hallucinogens.*

It is apparent that the statute neglects the pharmacological bases for defining a drug a narcotic because it seems to ignore the distinction between drugs that lead to physiological dependence and those that do not. For example, the opiates do have ad-

TABLE XXXV—NEW YORK

Citation	Type of Drug	Possession	Possession with Intent to Sell	Sale or Similar Transactions	Sale to Minor by Adult
N.Y. Penal Law Sec. 220 et seq. (Supp. 1970)	Dangerous Drug	6th degree Class A misdemeanor: NMT 1 year	Possession of a dangerous drug: 5th degree Class E felony, maximum 4 years, minimum set by parole board	Sale of a dangerous drug: 4th degree Class D felony, maximum 7 years, minimum set by parole board.	
	Narcotic Drug	4th Degree: 25 or more marihuana cigarettes, ⅛ ounce or more heroin or cocaine or ¼ ounce or more marihuana Class D felony, maximum 7 yrs. minimum fixed by parole board. 3rd Degree: 100 marihuana cigarettes, one or more ounces of		3rd Degree: sale of any narcotic drug: Class C felony, 5-15 years. 2nd Degree: sale consisting of 8 ounces or more of heroin, morphine, cocaine or raw opium: Class B felony, maximum 15-25 yrs., minimum 8⅓ years.	2nd Degree Sale Class B felony, maximum 15-25 yrs., minimum 8⅓ yrs.

heroin, morphine or cocaine, or one ounce of marihuana, or two or more ounces containing raw prepared opium—Class C felony, 5-15 years.
2nd Degree: 8 ounces or more of a narcotic drug—Class B felony 8⅓ yrs.-25 yrs.
1st Degree: 16 ounces or more of a narcotic drug (heroin, morphine, cocaine, opium)—Class A felony, 15 yrs.-life.

1st Degree: sale of one pound or more of heroin, cocaine, morphine or opium: Class A felony, minimum 15-25 yrs., maximum, life.

1st = 1st offense.
2nd = 2nd offense.
3rd = 3rd offense.
S = Subsequent offense.
NMT = Not more than.
NLT = Not less than.

TABLE XXXVI—NORTH CAROLINA

Citation	Type of Drug	General Penalty Provisions	Possession	Possession for Sale	Sale and Similar Transactions	Sale to Minor by Adult	Other Offenses
N. C. Gen. Stat. 90-86 et seq. (Supp. 1969)	Narcotics (including Halluci- nogens and marihuana)	1st: NMT 5 yrs. and/or NMT $1,000, but if one gram or less of mari- huana, misde- meanor punish- able at dis- cretion of the Court 2nd: 5-10 yrs. and/or $2,000 S: 15 yrs.-life and NMT $3,000				10-20 yrs.	
	Barbiturates and Stimulant Drugs		1st: NMT 2 yrs. and/or $1,000 2nd: Felony punishable at discretion of the Court	1st: 6 mos.-5 yrs. S: 1-10 yrs.	1st: 6 mos.-5 yrs. S: 1-10 yrs.		Conspiracy: to vio- late drug laws: 1st: NMT $1,000 and NMT 2 yrs. S: Felony

1st = 1st offense.
2nd = 2nd offense.
3rd = 3rd offense.
S = Subsequent offense.

NMT = Not more than.
NLT = Not less than.

diction-forming or addiction-sustaining liabilities but the hallu-cinogens are usually not the type of drugs which lead to physio-logical dependence. Apparently these drugs (narcotics and hal-lucinogens) are grouped together for the purpose of imposing similar penalties. Marihuana is also defined as a narcotic drug but less severe penalties are provided in instances involving the possession of one gram or less of marihuana. It is most signifi-cant that North Carolina continues to group marihuana and hal-lucinogenic substances as narcotics. A separate provision of the statute provides penalties for offenses involving the barbiturates and amphetamines. These penalties are less severe than those provided for narcotic drugs.

North Dakota: N.D. Cent. Code, Sec. 19-03-1 (Supp. 1970)

North Dakota has adopted the Uniform Controlled Substances Act which is similar to the *Federal Drug Abuse Prevention and Control Act of 1970.* The act adopted by North Dakota is also similar to the Uniform Controlled Substances Law enacted in Louisiana, Maryland, Mississippi and New Jersey.

The North Dakota law has classified the controlled substances into five schedules. In making a determination regarding a sub-stance, the state laboratories department is directed to consider the following:

1. the actual or relative potential for abuse;
2. the scientific evidence of its pharmacological effect, if known;
3. the state of current scientific knowledge regarding the sub-stance;
4. the history and current pattern of abuse;
5. the scope, duration, and significance of abuse;
6. the risk to the public health;
7. the potential of the substance to produce psychic or phys-iological dependence liability; and
8. whether the substance is an immediate precursor of a sub-stance already controlled.

Schedule I contains substances which have been found to have a high potential for abuse and no accepted medical use in the United States. The drugs within this category are 43 opiates (opi-ates are defined substances having an addiction forming or ad-

TABLE XXXVII—NORTH DAKOTA

Citation	Type of Drug	Possession	Possession With Intent to Sell or Deliver	Sale and Similar Transaction, Manufacture or Deliver	Sale to Minor by Adult
Uniform Controlled Substances Act N.D. Cent. Code Sec. 19-03.1 (Supp. 1970)	Schedule I: 42 opiates 22 opium derivatives (including heroin), 17 hallucinogens including DMT, LSD, Mescaline, Peyote, marihuana, Psilocybin and tetrahydrocannabinols	1st: NMT 5 yrs. and/or NMT $2,500 Except Marihuana: 1st: NMT 1 yr. and/or $500 S: NMT 10 yrs. and/or NMT $5,000 Except Marihuana: NMT 1 yr. and/or $500	Same as Sale	Narcotic: 1st: NMT 20 yrs. and/or NMT $10,000 S: NMT 40 yrs. and/or NMT $20,000 Non-narcotic: 1st: NMT 10 yrs. and/or $5,000 S: NMT 20 yrs. and/or $10,000	Narcotic: 1st: NMT 40 yrs. and/or $20,000 S: NMT twice the punishment of first offense Non-narcotic: 1st: NMT 20 yrs. and/or $10,000 S: NMT 40 yrs. and/or $40,000
	Schedule II: (including opium, opium poppy and straw, coca leaves and 21 specific opiates)	1st: NMT 5 yrs. and/or NMT $2,500 S: NMT 10 yrs. and/or NMT $5,000	Same as Sale	Narcotic: 1st: NMT 20 yrs. and/or NMT $10,000 S: NMT 40 yrs. and/or NMT $20,000 Non-narcotic: 1st: NMT 10 yrs. and/or NMT $10,000	Narcotic: 1st: NMT 40 yrs. and/or $20,000 S: NMT twice the punishment of the first offense Non-narcotic: 1st: NMT 40 yrs. and/or $20,000 S: NMT 40 yrs. and/or $40,000

Schedule III: (including amphetamine and its salts, phenmetrazine, methamphetamine, methylphenidate and derivatives of babituric acid and specific depressants and some materials and compounds containing limited quantities of narcotic drugs)	1st: NMT 5 yrs. and/or NMT $2,500 S: NMT 10 yrs. and/or NMT $5,000	Same as Sale	1st: NMT 10 yrs. and/or NMT $5,000 S: NMT 20 yrs. and/or $10,000	1st: NMT 20 yrs. and/or NMT $10,000 S: NMT 40 yrs. and/or NMT $20,000
Schedule IV: 13 enumerated depressants	1st: NMT 5 yrs. and/or NMT $2,500 S: NMT 10 yrs. and/or NMT $5,000	Same as Sale	1st: NMT 5 yrs. and/or NMT $2,500 S: NMT 10 yrs. and/or NMT $5,000	1st: NMT 10 yrs. and/or NMT $5,000 S: NMT 20 yrs. and/or NMT $10,000
Schedule V: Compounds and preparations containing limited amounts of narcotic drugs and one or more non-narcotic medical ingredients	1st: NMT 5 yrs. and/or NMT $2,500 S: NMT 10 yrs. and/or NMT $5,000	Same as Sale	1st: NMT 1 yr. and/or NMT $1,000 S: NMT 2 yrs. and/or NMT $2,000	1st: NMT 2 yrs. and/or NMT $2,000 S: NMT 4 yrs. and/or NMT $4,000

1st = 1st offense.
2nd = 2nd offense.

3rd = 3rd offense.
S = Subsequent offense.

NMT = Not more than.
NLT = Not less than.

diction sustaining liability similar to morphine or being capable of conversion into a drug having addiction forming or addiction sustaining liability), 22 opium derivatives (including heroin) and 17 hallucinogenic substances. The hallucinogenic substances include dimethyltryptamine (DMT), lysergic acid diethylamide (LSD), marihuana, mescaline, peyote, psilocybin and tetrahydrocannabinols. It is significant to note that marihuana is grouped as an hallucinogenic substance not as a narcotic substance. In defining "narcotic drug" the statute includes opium and opiate, opium poppy and poppy straw and coca leaves (cocaine).

The definition of "narcotic drug" gathers importance because the statute provides different penalties for drugs classified in Schedule I based on whether or not the drug is a narcotic. For example, a first offense involving the unlawful manufacture or delivery of an opium derivative such as heroin is punishable by imprisonment of not more than 20 years and/or not more than $10,000. However, a first offense involving the unlawful manufacture or sale of a non-narcotic drug in Schedule I is punishable by not more than 10 years and/or not more than $10,000. Possession offenses involving marihuana include penalties which are notably less severe than possession offenses involving other controlled substances. The possession of marihuana is punishable by not more than one year imprisonment and/or $500.

The controlled substances which are classified under Schedules I-V are evaluated in terms of their potential for abuse relative to other controlled substances and the degree to which they lead to physiological or psychological dependence.

The act provides for conditional discharge of the proceedings against first offenders who are charged with unlawful possession of controlled substances. However, the act does not have a provision similar to that of the federal act which provides for criminal records being expunged in cases involving youthful offenders.

Ohio: Ohio Rev. Code, Sec. 3719.01. et seq. Supp. (1970)

The Ohio drug abuse laws establish three categories of dangerous drugs for purposes of imposing penalties for drug related

TABLE XXXVIII—OHIO

Citation	Type of Drug	Unlawful Manufacture or Unlawful Procurement	Possession	Possession With Intent to Sell	Sale and Similar Transactions	Sale to Minor	Other Offenses
Ohio Rev. Code Sec. 3719.01 (Supp. 1970)	Narcotic Drug	1st: 2-5 yrs. and NMT $10,000 2nd: 5-10 yrs. and NMT $10,000 S: 10-20 yrs. and NMT $10,000	1st: 2-5 yrs. and NMT $10,000 2nd: 5-10 yrs. and NMT $10,000 S: 10-20 yrs. and NMT $10,000	1st: 10-20 yrs. 2nd: 15-30 yrs. S: 20-40 yrs.	1st: 20-40 yrs.	1st: 30-life	Carnal Knowledge of another person knowing that such person is under the influence of a narcotic drug.
Ohio Rev. Code 3719.40 et seq. (Supp. 1970)	Hallucinogens: DMT, LSD, Peyote, Mescaline and marihuana	1st: 2-15 yrs. and NMT $10,000 2nd: 5-20 yrs. and NMT $10,000 S: 10-30 yrs. and NMT $10,000	1st: NMT 1 yr. and/or $1,000 S: 1-10 yrs.	1st: 10-20 yrs. 2nd: 15-30 yrs. S: 20-40 yrs.	1st: 10-20 yrs. 2nd: 15-30 yrs. S: 20-40 yrs.	1st: 30-life	1st: 2-15 yrs. & NMT $10,000 2nd: 5-20 yrs. and NMT $10,000 S: 10-30 yrs. and NMT $10,000
	Barbiturates		1st: NMT 1 yr. and/or $1,000 S: NMT 10 yrs. and/or $1,000	1st: 1-5 yrs. or NMT $1,000 S: 2-20 yrs. and/or $5,000	1st: 1-5 yrs. or NMT $1,000 S: 2-20 yrs. and/or $5,000	1st: 1-5 yrs. or NMT $1,000 S: 2-20 yrs. and/or $5,000	Inducing minors to violate narcotic laws 1st: 10-25 yrs. 2nd: 25-50 yrs.

1st = 1st offense.
2nd = 2nd offense.

3rd = 3rd offense.
S = Subsequent offense.

NMT = Not more than.
NLT = Not less than.

offenses. The first group of controlled substances are the narcotics. Narcotics are defined as coca leaves (cocaine), opium, Isonipecaine, Amidone, isamidone, and ketobemidone. Marihuana is expressly excluded from this category.

The second group of controlled substances are hallucinogens which include lysergic acid diethylamide (LSD), dimethyltryptamine (DMT), cannabis, psilocybin, mescaline, peyote and other substances which produce hallucinations or illusions when introduced into the body. Here again it may be noted that in some states marihuana is classified as an hallucinogenic substance and in others it is considered a narcotic drug. Since the penalties vary for offenses involving these drugs, a scientific basis for classification should be established.

The third group of controlled substances are the barbiturates and amphetamines. Penalties imposed for offenses involving these dangerous substances are less severe than those imposed for offenses involving the narcotic drugs and hallucinogens.

A unique provision in the Ohio law makes it unlawful to have carnal knowledge with any person if there is knowledge that the person is under the influence of a narcotic drug.

Oklahoma: Okla. Stat. Ann. Tit. 63 Sec. 401 et seq.
(Supp. 1969)

Oklahoma has divided the regulated substances into three separate categories for purposes of imposing penalties. The first category is *narcotic drugs* which include coca leaves (cocaine), opium and its derivatives, Isonipecaine, Amidone, isoamidone and keto-bemidone. Marihuana is not included in the definition of narcotic drugs. Title 63 Sec. 470.11 of the Oklahoma statutes provides that "an 'addict' to narcotic drugs or marihuana means any person. . . ." This is of particular significance because if the Oklahoma legislature feels that marihuana does have an addiction sustaining liability it should be included within the definition of narcotics. However, marihuana appears in a separate category of the statute and the penalties for offenses involving marihuana have more severe maximum sentences than offenses involving narcotic drugs. If the penalty invoked is to be commensurate with the dangers inherent in the regulated substance,

TABLE XXXIX—OKLAHOMA

Citation	Type of Drug	General Penalty Provisions	Addiction	Possession	Possession for Sale	Sale or Similar Transaction	Sale to Minor by Adult
Okla. Stat. Ann. Tit. 63, Sec. 401 et seq. (Supp. 1969)	Narcotics (including coca leaves [cocaine], and opium derivatives)	1st: NMT $1,000 and/or NMT 5 yrs. 2nd: NMT $3,000 and/or 5-10 yrs. S: NMT $5,000 or 10-20 yrs.	1st: NLT 90 days S: NLT 6 mos.	Same as General Penalty Provisions	Same as General Penalty Provisions	Same as General Penalty Provisions	Selling or giving heroin to a minor, 10 yrs.-death in the electric chair
	Marihuana	1st and S: NMT 7 yrs. and/or $5,000	1st: NLT 90 days S: NLT 6 mos.	Same as General Penalty Provisions	Same as General Penalty Provisions	Same as General Penalty Provisions	1st: NMT 20 yrs. S: 5 yrs. to life
	Barbiturates and Stimulants (included are: barbiturates, amphetamines and hallucinogenic substances)	1st: NMT 1 yr. and/or $500 S: NMT 2 yrs. and/or $1,000	1st: NLT 90 days S: NLT 6 mos.	Same as General Penalty Provisions	Same as General Penalty Provisions	1st and S: NMT 5 yrs. and/or $1,000	

1st = 1st offense.
2nd = 2nd offense.

3rd = 3rd offense.
S = Subsequent offense.

NMT = Not more than.
NLT = Not less than.

the Oklahoma statute appears to have lost touch with established pharmacological criteria.

The third category of drugs set forth in the statute are the barbiturates and stimulants. This category also contains some questionable definitions. A 1968 amendment which defines barbiturates provides that barbiturate means "the salts and derivatives of barbituric acid or compounds, preparations or mixtures thereof which the Division of Health shall find and declare by rule or regulation duly promulgated after reasonable public notice and opportunity for hearing to have a *hypnotic or somnifacient effect on the body of a human or animal.* Most other states define barbiturates as substances which have a depressant effect upon the central nervous system. A 1959 amendment to the Oklahoma statutes defined stimulants as those drugs, salts, mixtures, or optical isomers having a stimulating effect on the central nervous system. However, in 1968 the legislature amended this definition in an effort to control the wave of abuse involving the hallucinogenic substances. Therefore, in defining stimulant drugs, and in prescribing penalties for offenses involving these substances, the legislature expanded the definition of "stimulant drugs" to include lysergic acid diethylamide (LSD), dimethyltryptamine (DMT) and psilocybin. This is a departure from the classification in most other states which seem to classify stimulants and hallucinogenic substances separately.

An Oklahoma statute also provides that it is a crime to be an "addict." For purposes of the act, an "addict" to narcotic drugs or marihuana means any person showing a medical need for a narcotic drug or losing the power of self-control with reference to the use of narcotic drugs or any person who habitually uses marihuana. The penalty prescribed for a person who is an addict is confinement in the county jail for a term not less than six months. This provision which makes it a crime to be a narcotic addict is virtually non-enforceable because of the decision by the United States Supreme Court in the case of *Robinson v. California* (370 U.S. 660, 8 L.Ed.2d 758, 82 S. Ct. 1417 [1962]). In *Robinson v. California* the Supreme Court of the United States held a California statute making it a misdemeanor for a person to "be addicted to the use of narcotics," unconstitutional.

TABLE XL—OREGON

Citation	Type of Drug	General Penalty Provisions	Possession
Ore. Rev. Stat. Sec. 474.010 et seq. (1969)	Narcotics: coca leaves, opium and marihuana	All narcotics except marihuana: NMT 10 years and/or $10,000. Marihuana: Imprisonment in county jail for NMT 1 year and/or $5,000 fine or imprisonment in penitentiary for NMT 10 years and/or $5,000	
	Dangerous Drugs: Drugs included in published regulations of the State Board of Pharmacy	NMT 1 year in county jail and/or $5,000, and/or NMT 10 years in state penitentiary and/or $5,000	NMT one year in county jail and/or $500

1st = 1st offense.
2nd = 2nd offense.
3rd = 3rd offense.
S = Subsequent offense.
NMT = Not more than.
NLT = Not less than.

The California statute provided that a person was guilty of this offense whether or not he has ever used or possessed any narcotics within the State. The Supreme Court of the United States held that addiction to narcotics is similar to having a disease, and it is a violation of the constitutional prohibition of cruel and unusual punishment to punish a person for being addicted to narcotic drugs.

Oregon: Ore. Rev. Stat. Sec. 474.10 et seq. (1969)

Oregon has very general provisions for offenses involving controlled substances. The general penalty provisions seem to maximize the discretion of the court when sentence is imposed. The statute providing penalties groups the unlawful acts involving the controlled drugs, and the court imposes sentence based upon the general penalty provisions. Although the statute classifies drugs as either narcotic drugs (including marihuana) and dangerous drugs, the maximum sentences set by statute for offenses involving all these drugs are similar. However, the court probably tailors the sentence to fit the type of offense and the type of drug involved. This, of course, subjects a defendant to the whims and caprices of the particular judge.

Pennsylvania: Pa. Stat. Tit. 35 Sec. 780-1 et seq. (Supp. 1970)

The Pennsylvania statutes recognize two broad categories of drugs. The Secretary of Health of the Commonwealth of Pennsylvania is authorized to classify drugs as either narcotic drugs or dangerous drugs. Narcotic drugs include opium, cocaine, marihuana, Isonipecaine and drugs which are found to have an addiction forming or addiction sustaining liability similar to morphine or cocaine.

The dangerous drugs are defined as those drugs other than narcotic drugs and include barbiturates, amphetamines and any drug which because of its toxicity or other potentiality for harmful effect are found not to be safe for use except under the supervision of a practitioner licensed by law to administer such drug.

The broad categories in the Pennsylvania statute leave much room for discretion when sentence is imposed for violations of the drug related offenses.

TABLE XLI—PENNSYLVANIA

Citation	Type of Drug	General Penalty Provisions	Possession	Sale
Pa. Stat. Tit. 35 Sec. 780-1 et seq. (Supp. 1970)	Narcotics		1st: 2-5 years and NMT $2,000 2nd: 5-10 years and NMT $5,000 S: 10-30 years and NMT $7,500	1st: 5-20 years and NMT $5,000 2nd: 10-30 years and NMT $15,000 3rd: Life and NMT $30,000
	Dangerous Drugs	1st: NMT one year and/or NMT $5,000 S: NMT 3 years and/or $25,000		

1st = 1st offense.
2nd = 2nd offense.

3rd = 3rd offense.
S = Subsequent offense.

NMT = Not more than.
NLT = Not less than.

Possession of narcotic drugs is treated harshly. A first offense is punishable by two to five years imprisonment and not more than a $2,000 fine. A second offense is punishable by five to ten years imprisonment and not more than a $5,000 fine. A subsequent offense is punishable by imprisonment of 10 to 30 years and not more than $7,500. These penalties for offenses involving possession of narcotic drugs, including marihuana, are quite harsh compared to penalties imposed for possession offenses in other states and under the federal law.

Rhode Island: R.I. Gen. Laws Ann. Sec. 21-28-1 et seq. (Supp. 1969)

Rhode Island has enacted two statutes directed at controlling drug abuse. The Uniform Narcotic Drug Act of Rhode Island provides that it is unlawful for any person to manufacture, possess, have under his control, sell, prescribe, administer, dispense or compound any narcotic drug except as authorized in the statute. Narcotic drugs include cocaine, opium, cannabis and the *hallucinogenic drugs* such as mescaline, peyote, lysergic acid diethylamide and psilocybin and any other drug which is determined to have an addiction sustaining or an addiction forming liability. The Rhode Island definition of narcotics is unique because it *includes the hallucinogens* within the definition of narcotics. This may be practical from the standpoint of providing harsh penalties for the unlawful manufacture, possession or sale of these harmful substances but the hallucinogenic substances cannot be considered addiction sustaining from a pharmacological standpoint. There is a possibility that a drug may be placed within this category which does have a potential for abuse but is not actually a narcotic drug. This would result in harsh penalties imposed for an offense involving unlawful possession as a consequence of an improper classification determination. Often the harsh penalty imposed for an offense involving unlawful possession has its origin in an initial improper grouping of a substance which has a potential for abuse.

The second act which aims at controlling drug abuse is the "Rhode Island Barbiturate and Central Nervous System Stimulant Act." This act defines barbiturates as not only the salts and

TABLE XLII—RHODE ISLAND

Citation	Type of Drug	General Penalty Provisions	Possession	Possession With Intent to Sell	Sale	Sale to Minor
R.I. Gen. Laws Ann. Sec. 21-28-1 et seq. (Supp. 1969)	Narcotics (Including marihuana and hallucinogens)	NMT 1 yr. and/ or $1,000	1st: 2-15 yrs. and NMT $10,000 2nd: 5-20 yrs. and NMT $10,000 S: 10-30 yrs. and NMT $10,000	1st: 10-20 yrs. 2nd: 15-30 yrs. S: 20-40 yrs.	1st and S: 20-40 yrs.	30 yrs. to life (no benefit of probation)
R.I. Gen. Laws Ann. Sec. 21-29-1 et seq. (Supp. 1969)	Barbiturates and Hypnotic Drugs	1st: NMT 2 yrs. and/or $1,000 S: NMT 5 yrs. and/or NMT $5,000	1st: NMT 2 yrs. and/or $1,000 S: NMT 5 yrs. and/or NMT $5,000		1st: NMT 20 yrs. S: 5 yrs. to life	

1st = 1st offense.
2nd = 2nd offense.

3rd = 3rd offense.
S = Subsequent offense.

NMT = Not more than.
NLT = Not less than.

derivatives of barbituric acid but also hypnotic or somnifacient drugs, whether or not derivatives of barbituric acid. The words "central nervous stimulants" mean amphetamine and desoxyephedrine and their derivatives. It is difficult to understand why the offenses involving the central nervous system drugs and the barbiturates should not be treated as harshly as the narcotic substances which include the hallucinogens.

South Carolina: S.C. Code Ann., Sec. 32-1050 et seq. (Supp. 1970); S.C. Code Ann., Sec. 32-1462 et seq. (Supp. 1970)

The legislation directed at controlling drug abuse in South Carolina reflects the difficulty of classifying drugs. The statutes attempt to classify the dangerous substances as either narcotic or depressant, stimulant and counterfeit drugs. Because the statute lacks a precise definition of these types of drugs, it is difficult to ascertain which of the two categories the hallucinogenic substances will fall under. Section 32-1492.1 of the statute refers to the unlawful sale of certain drugs. This section provides that "it is unlawful for any person to sell, offer for sale or possess for sale any cocaine, alpha- or beta-eucaine, opium, morphine, heroin, Isonipecaine, marihuana, LSD or other *narcotics* or drugs of like character or their compounds." This indicates that LSD is considered a narcotic drug for purposes of invoking penalties for unlawful sales.

The confusion which occurs when drugs are classified is further reflected in Section 32-1505 which defines depressant or stimulant drugs. This section provides that the term "depressant or stimulant drug" means ". . . any drug which contains any quantity of a substance which the State Board of Health or the appropriate federal drug authorities have found to have, and by regulation designated as having a potential for abuse because of its depressant or stimulant effect on the central nervous system *or its hallucinogenic effect.*" Since the definition includes drugs which contain substances which have an hallucinogenic effect LSD would be included in this category. However, in an effort to deal with the wave of abuse involving LSD, the legislature provided a penalty for unlawful sales which is equivalent to the penalties invoked for narcotic offenses. Although this deterrent

TABLE XLIII—SOUTH CAROLINA

Citation	Type of Drug	General Penalty Provisions	Possession	Possession With Intent to Sell	Sale	Sale to a Minor
S.C. Code Ann. Sec. 32-1462 et seq. (Supp. 1970)	Narcotics (including LSD and Marihuana)	1st: NMT 2 yrs. and/or NMT $2,000 2nd: 2-5 yrs. and/or $2,000 to $5,000 S: 10-20 yrs.	1st: NMT 2 yrs. and/or NMT $2,000 2nd: 2-5 yrs. and/or $2,000 to $5,000 S: 10-20 yrs.	1st: 3½ yrs. and/ or $3,500 2nd: 5 yrs. S: 10 yrs. (no probation for 2nd and S)	1st: 3½ yrs. and/or $3,500 2nd: 5 yrs. S: 10 yrs. (no probation for 2nd and S offense)	1st: 5 yrs. and/or $5,000 S: 10 yrs. (no probation or suspended sentence for S offenses)
S.C. Code Ann. Sec. 32-1050 et seq. (Supp. 1970)	Depressant, stimulant, counterfeit drugs	1st: NMT 2 yrs. and/or $2,000 2nd: 2-5 yrs. and/or $2,000 to $5,000 S: 5-10 yrs.				

1st = 1st offense.
2nd = 2nd offense.
3rd = 3rd offense.
S = Subsequent offense.
NMT = Not more than.
NLT = Not less than.

effect is commendable, it would have been preferable not to group LSD with narcotic drugs because it is not a narcotic. Furthermore, there is little need to classify the drug. The sale could have been prohibited without referring to the drug as a narcotic substance or hallucinogenic substance.

It is significant to note that unlawful sales of narcotic drugs are not punished as harshly as in most other states. There is little statutory difference between punishment invoked for narcotic possession offenses and punishment invoked for unlawful sales of narcotic drugs. Offenses involving depressant, stimulant and counterfeit drugs are punished by general penalty provisions which, therefore, places a large amount of discretion in the sentencing court.

South Dakota: S.D. Sec. 39-17-44 et seq. (Supp. 1971)

South Dakota enacted the State Drugs and Substances Control Act in 1970. This act is similar to the *Federal Drug Abuse Prevention and Control Act of 1970* and the Uniform Controlled Substances Act adopted by Louisiana, Maryland and Mississippi. The South Dakota act classifies the drugs into four schedules. This is in contrast to the federal act which classifies the drugs into five schedules. The criteria that the Commissioner of Drugs and Substances Control uses in determining which schedule a substance is classified in is:

(1) The substance's actual or relative potential for abuse;
(2) Scientific evidence of its pharmacological effect, if known;
(3) The state of current scientific knowledge regarding the substance;
(4) The history of the substance and its current pattern of abuse;
(5) The scope, duration, and significance of abuse;
(6) What, if any, risk there is to public health;
(7) Its psychic or physiological dependence potential or liability;
(8) Whether the substance is an immediate precursor of a substance already controlled; and

(9) Its other uses, both medical and commercial.

These criteria are similar to the considerations set forth in the federal act.

The possession of drugs classified in Schedule I or II is punished more severely than under the federal law. It is difficult to understand why the drugs are classified in Schedules I or II because offenses involving drugs grouped in these two categories are punished similarly. The basic distinction between the two schedules is that the substances in Schedule I have no recognized medical use, but the Schedule II drugs have a currently recognized medical use. This is a superficial distinction, though, since similar penalties attach for offenses involving substances in either Schedule I or II. There is a significant difference between this act and the federal act, where penalties are imposed for offenses involving drugs grouped in Schedule I or II. Under the federal law, in addition to determining whether the drug is classified in Schedule I or II, there is a secondary consideration of whether the drug is a narcotic. The South Dakota law does not take into consideration whether the drug is a narcotic or a non-narcotic for purposes of imposing sentence as long as it is a Schedule I or II drug.

The South Dakota act does contain a provision which permits a reduced penalty for a first offense of illegal possession of marihuana even though marihuana is grouped with the hallucinogenic substances in Schedule I.

There is a provision in the South Dakota act, granting authority to the sentencing court to place a first offender on probation. However, the act does not contain a provision similar to the federal act which provides that the criminal records of minors be expunged upon satisfaction of probationary terms.

Tennessee: Tenn. Code Ann. Sec. 52-1201 et seq. (Supp. 1969); Tenn. Code Ann. Sec. 52-1301 et seq. (Supp. 1969)

The laws of Tennessee classify drugs within the category of narcotics, barbital or legend drugs. Narcotic drugs include coca leaves, opium, Isonipecaine, Amidone, osoamidone, and keto-bemidone and every substance neither chemically nor physically

TABLE XLIV—SOUTH DAKOTA

Citation	Type of Drug	Possession	Possession With Intent to Sell	Sale	Sale to Minors
Sec. 39-17-44 et seq. (Supp. 1971)	Schedule I: 42 specific substances, 17 opium derivatives (including heroin), 12 hallucinogenic substances (including LSD, marihuana, mescaline, peyote, psilocybin and tetrahydrocannabinols)	1st: NMT 5 yrs. and/or NMT $5,000 2nd: NMT 15 yrs. and/or $15,000 S: NMT 40 yrs. and/or $20,000 Except one ounce or less of marihuana: NMT 1 yr. and/or $500	Same as Sale	1st: NMT 10 yrs. and/or NMT $5,000 2nd: NMT 15 yrs. and/or $10,000 S: NMT 40 yrs. and/or $20,000	Twice the punishment authorized for ordinary sale.
	Schedule II: Opium, coca leaves, opiate and derivatives not referred to in Schedule I and 20 specific opiates	1st: NMT 5 yrs. and/or NMT $5,000 2nd: NMT 15 yrs. and/or $15,000 S: NMT 40 yrs. and/or $20,000	Same as Sale	1st: NMT 10 yrs. and/or NMT $5,000 2nd: NMT 15 yrs. and/or $10,000 S: NMT 40 yrs. and/or $20,000	Twice the punishment authorized for ordinary sale.

	Sale	Possession		
Schedule III: Stimulants, including amphetamine, phemetrazine. Depressants: Barbiturates and 15 substances with a depressant effect on central nervous system	1st: 5 yrs. and/or $5,000 2nd: NMT 15 yrs. and/or $15,000 S: NMT 40 yrs. and/or $20,000	Same as Sale	1st: NMT 5 yrs. and/or $5,000 2nd: NMT 15 yrs. and/or $15,000 3rd: NMT 40 yrs. and/or $20,000	Twice the punishment authorized for ordinary sale.
Schedule IV: Compounds, mixtures, or preparations containing limited quantities of narcotic drugs mixed with non-narcotic medicinal ingredients	1st: NMT 5 yrs. and/or $5,000 2nd: NMT 15 yrs. and/or $15,000 S: NMT 40 yrs. and/or $20,000	Same as Sale	1st: NMT 2 yrs and/or $5,000 2nd: 4 yrs. and/or $10,000 S: 8 yrs. and $20,000	Twice the punishment authorized for ordinary sale.

1st = 1st offense.
2nd = 2nd offense.
3rd = 3rd offense.
S = Subsequent offense.

NMT = Not more than.
NLT = Not less than.

TABLE XLV—TENNESSEE

Citation	Types of Drugs	General Penalty Provisions	Possession	Possession With Intent to Sell	Sale
Tenn. Code Ann. Sec. 52-1301 et seq. (Supp. 1969)	Narcotics (including marihuana)	1st: 2-5 yrs. and $500 2nd: 5-10 yrs. and $500 3rd: 10-20 yrs. and $500 (no suspension of sentence after 1st offense)	1st: 2-5 yrs. and $500 2nd: 5-10 yrs. and $500 3rd: 10-20 yrs. and $500 (no suspension of sentence after 1st offense)	Same as Possession	Same as Possession
Tenn. Code Ann. Sec. 52-1201 et seq. (Supp. 1969)	Barbital and legend drugs	1st: 1-5 yrs. and/or NMT $500 S: 1-5 yrs. and/or NMT $500			

1st = 1st offense.
2nd = 2nd offense.
3rd = 3rd offense.
S = Subsequent offense.

NMT = Not more than.
NLT = Not less than.

distinguishable from them. The definition of narcotics does not include marihuana, but the offenses involving marihuana are punished in the same manner as those involving narcotics. The narcotic drug law of Tennessee merely provides general penalty provisions for drug related offenses. This is in contrast to the varied penalties imposed in other states after considering the seriousness of the offense. The unlawful possession of a regulated substance should not be punished as harshly as the sale of a regulated substance to a minor.

The second category of regulated substances is referred to in Tennessee as barbital and legend drugs. Barbital is defined as including the salts of barbituric acid, or any compound, derivatives or mixtures that may be used for producing hypnotic or somnifacient effects. The term *legend drugs* means and includes amphetamines, desoxyephedrine or compounds or mixtures thereof and other substances having a stimulating effect upon the central nervous system. It is significant to note that the Tennessee statute makes no specific reference to the hallucinogenic substances.

Texas: Tex. Pen. Code Art. 725(b), Art. 726(d) (Supp. 1970)

Texas classifies regulated substances as narcotics or dangerous drugs. The narcotic drugs include opium, cocaine, cannabis, Amidone, Isonipecaine, and opiates. Opiates are defined as any drug found to have an addiction forming or addiction sustaining liability similar to opium or cocaine. It is important to note that in Texas marihuana is included in the category of narcotic drugs. The unlawful possession of a narcotic drug is punishable by imprisonment of two years to life for a first offense. Therefore a first offender unlawfully possessing marihuana may be punished by life imprisonment. In contrast to the unlawful possession of a narcotic drug, the possession of an hallucinogenic substance in Texas is punished by 30 days to two years imprisonment and/or not more than $3,000. This should well illustrate the importance of classifying drugs pursuant to well defined guidelines. Under the federal act and the states which have adopted the Uniform Controlled Substance Act, marihuana is classified as an hallucinogenic substance. If it is an hallucinogenic substance it should be

TABLE XLVI—TEXAS

Citation	Type of Drug	General Penalty Provisions	Possession	Sale	Sale to a Minor
Tex. Pen. Code Art. 725(b) (Supp. 1969-70)	Narcotic (including marihuana)	1st: 2 yrs. to life S: 10 yrs. to life No probation or suspended sentence after 1st offense	1st: 2 yrs. to life S: 10 yrs. to life No probation or suspended sentence after 1st offense	1st: 5 yrs. to life S: 10 yrs. to life No probation or suspended sentence after 1st offense	1st: 5 yrs. to life S: 10 yrs. to life, possible death sentence No probation or suspended sentence after 1st offense
Tex. Pen. Code Art. 726(d) (Supp. 1969-70)	Dangerous Drugs: Stimulants, depressants and hallucinogenic substances (including LSD)	1st: 30 days to 2 yrs. and/or NMT $3,000 S: 2-10 yrs.	1st: 30 days to 2 yrs. and/or NMT $3,000 S: 2-10 yrs. But possession of methamphetamine is punished by 2-10 years for the first offense	1st and S: 2-10 years	1st and S: 10 yrs. to life

1st = 1st offense.
2nd = 2nd offense.

3rd = 3rd offense.
S   = Subsequent offense.

NMT = Not more than.
NLT = Not less than.

classified accordingly in the Texas statute. The improper classification of controlled substances results in penalties which are grossly disproportionate to the relative dangers of the controlled substances. The Texas experience with classification should illustrate the need for a well-defined classification approach.

The second category of controlled substances in Texas is dangerous drugs. These drugs include the amphetamines, barbiturate and hallucinogenic substances within the definition of dangerous drugs so as to prevent the unlawful manufacture, sale or possession of lysergic acid diethylamide (LSD), methamphetamine, dimethyltryptamine, psilocybin, peyote, and mescaline and others. Unlawful possession of a dangerous drug is punished by 30 days to two years and a fine of not more than $3,000 for a first offense. However, the statute specifically aims at deterring the use of methamephetamine as evidenced by the fact that although it is classified as a dangerous drug unlawful possession is punished by imprisonment of not less than two nor more than ten years.

There is no apparent reason why the possession of narcotic drugs should be punished more harshly than possession of the dangerous drugs especially since the classifications are not the consequence of well-defined criteria for categorizing harmful substances. There is no substantial reason why offenses involving LSD should be punished so much less severely than offenses involving marihuana.

Utah: Utah Code Ann. Sec. 58-37-1 (Supp. 1971)

Utah has enacted the Utah Controlled Substances Act. The act is similar to that of Louisiana, Maryland, Mississippi and New Jersey which have adopted the *Federal Drug Abuse Prevention and Control Act of 1970*. The Utah act follows the distinction made under the federal act for narcotic and non-narcotic substances within Schedule I and II. However, offenses involving marihuana are punished the same as offenses involving Schedule IV drugs. If the purpose of classifying drugs is to impose penalties proportionate to the inherent dangers of the controlled substances, it is contrary to this purpose to classify drugs in one

TABLE XLVII—UTAH

Citation	Type of Drug	Possession	Possession With Intent to Sell	Sale or Distribution*	Sale to a Minor
Utah Code Ann. Sec. 58-37-1 (1971 Supp.)	Schedule I: 42 opiates, 22 opium derivatives, 17 hallucinogens	1st: 6 mos. and/or $299; 2nd: 1 yr. and/or $1,000; S: NMT 5 yrs.	Same as Sale	Narcotic: 1st: NMT 15 yrs. and/or $15,000; Marihuana: 1st: NMT 5 yrs. and/or $5,000; S**; Non-narcotic: 1st: NMT 10 yrs. and/or $10,000 or both	Narcotic: 1st: NMT 20 yrs. and/or $15,000; S***; Non-narcotic: 1st: NMT 15 yrs. and/or $10,000; S***; Marihuana: 1st: NMT 10 yrs. and/or $5,000
	Schedule II: opium, opiate, cocaine, 21 opiates	1st: 6 mos. and/or $299; 2nd: 1 yr. and/or $1,000; S: NMT 5 years	Same as Sale	Narcotic: 1st: NMT 15 yrs. and/or NMT $15,000; Non-narcotic: 1st: NMT 10 yrs. and/or $10,000; S**	Narcotic: 1st: NMT 20 yrs. and/or $15,000; Non-narcotic: 1st: NMT 15 yrs. and/or $10,000; S***

Schedule III: Barbiturates, Stimulants	1st: 6 mos. and/or $299 2nd: 1 yr. and/or $1,000 S: NMT 5 years	Same as Sale	1st: NMT 10 yrs. and/or $10,000 S**	1st: NMT 15 yrs. and/or $10,000 S**
Schedule IV: Depressants, Stimulants	1st: 6 mos. and/or $299 2nd: 1 yr. and/or $1,000 S: NMT 5 years	Same as Sale	1st: NMT 5 years and/or $5,000 or both S**	1st: NMT 10 yrs. and/or $5,000 S**
Schedule V: Mixtures and preparations containing small amounts of narcotics	1st: 6 mos. and/or $299 2nd: 1 yr. and/or $1,000 S: NMT 5 years	Same as Sale	1st: NMT 1 year and/or $1,000 S**	1st: NMT 10 yrs. and/or $5,000 S**

* If distribution is made without consideration, only one half the penalty is imposed.
** Subsequent offenses are punishable by one-half the maximum.

1st = 1st offense.	3rd = 3rd offense.	NMT = Not more than.
2nd = 2nd offense.	S = Subsequent offense.	NLT = Not less than.

TABLE XLVIII—VERMONT

Citation	Type of Drug	Possession	Possession With Intent to Sell	Sale	Sale to a Minor
Vt. Stat. Ann. Tit. 18, Sec. 4201 et seq. (Supp. 1970)	Marihuana or stimulant or depressant drug	1st: NMT 6 mos. and/or $500 S: NMT 2 yrs. and/or $2,000	1. 25 or more marihuana cigarettes; 2. Any compound or mixture containing more than ⅜ ounce of heroin, morphine or cocaine; 3. ½ ounce or more of marihuana; 4. ½ ounce or more of prepared opium; 5. 100 times the manufacturer's recommended maximum individual dose of a depressant or stimulant drug; 6. 500 micrograms or more of LSD: 50 milligrams or more of psilocybin; 700 milligrams or more of mescaline; 6 milligrams of methylphenylethamine; 200 milligrams of dimethytryptamine NMT 2 years and/or NMT $2,000	Sale of any regulated drug: 1st: NMT 5 yrs. and/or NMT $10,000 S: 10-25 yrs. and NMT $25,000	Sale of any regulated drug: 1st: NMT 5 yrs. and/or NMT $10,000 S: 10-25 yrs. and NMT $2,500

| Hallucinogenic or narcotic | 1st: NMT 1 yr. and/or $1,000 | 1. 100 or more marihuana cigarettes;
2. one or more ounces of heroin, morphine or cocaine;
3. two or more ounces of marihuana;
4. two or more ounces of raw or prepared opium;
5. 300 times the manufacturer's recommended individual dose of a depressant or stimulant drug;
6. 1,000 or more micrograms of LSD;
7. 100 milligrams or more of psilocybin, 700 milligrams or more of mescaline, 12 milligrams of methylphenylethylamine or 400 or more milligrams of diemethy-tryptamine
NMT 5 years and/or NMT $5,000 |

1st = 1st offense.
2nd = 2nd offense.
3rd = 3rd offense.
S = Subsequent offense.

NMT = Not more than.
NLT = Not less than.

category and then impose a penalty as if they were classified in another schedule.

Vermont: Vt. Stat. Ann. Tit. 18, Sec. 4201 et seq. (Supp. 1970)

Vermont has established three categories for regulated drugs. A controlled substance will be classified as a narcotic, an hallucinogen, or a stimulant or depressant drug. Although the definitions for each of these categories do have a tendency to overlap they are closer to pharmacological definitions than the definitions promulgated by most other states.

The narcotic drugs are defined as opium, coca leaves (cocaine), pethidine (Isonipecaine, meperidine) and opiates or their compounds, salts or derivatives. Marihuana is not included within the definition of narcotics.

The hallucinogens are defined as stromonium, mescaline or peyote, lysergic acid diethylamide, and psilocybin, and all synthetic equivalents of chemicals contained in resinous extractives of *cannabis sativa,* or any salts, or derivatives or compounds of any preparations or mixtures thereof, and any other substance which is designated as habit forming or as having a serious potential for abuse arising out of its effect on the central nervous system or its hallucinogenic effect. It is significant to note that the unlawful possession of an hallucinogenic substance involves the same penalty as the unlawful possession of a narcotic drug.

The category of the depressant or stimulant drugs is reserved for amphetamines, barbiturates or any drug the Vermont Board of Health designates as having a potential for abuse arising out of its effect upon the central nervous system.

Careful analysis of the Vermont statute indicates some very rational provisions. The possession of marihuana or a stimulant or depressant drug involves maximum penalties of six months imprisonment. However, the possession of a narcotic or an hallucinogenic substance is punished by imprisonment of up to one year. Apparently, the legislature has made an effort to deter the use of the drugs having greater harmful effects. This is an interesting reversal from those states which still define marihuana as a narcotic. In those states the possession of marihuana is usually punished quite harshly and in almost all instances more severely than the unlawful possession of an hallucinogen. In Texas, for example, the possession of marihuana is punishable by two years to life imprisonment for a first offense. The Texas statute, however, punishes the unlawful possession of a hallucinogenic substance by 30 days to two years imprisonment and a fine of not more than $3,000. This contrast between Texas punishing the unlawful possession of a hallucinogen less severely and Vermont punishing the same offense more severely than the possession of marihuana reflects the varied legislative attitudes in approaching the problems of drug abuse. However, it also indicates that the enactments are not in response to a consideration of objective pharmacological criteria.

The Vermont provisions relating to the sale of *any* regulated drug should not go unnoticed. This illustrates *the punishment of a criminal act,* the sale of a regulated drug, and does not pivot on a sophisticated schedule of drugs. Where the sale of a drug is involved the crime is no longer considered victimless and, therefore, the unlawful act should be punished harshly irrespective of the chemical nature of the drug.

Virginia: Va. Code Ann., Sec. 54-524.1 et seq. (Supp. 1970)

Virginia enacted the Drug Control Act of 1970. In some respects the act is similar to the *Federal Drug Abuse Prevention and Control Act of 1970.* The Virginia statute has adopted the federal approach which classifies the regulated substances into five schedules. However, an important distinction is evidenced by the fact that Virginia prescribes punishments for offenses involving the Schedule I or Schedule II drugs without considering whether the substance is a narcotic. Under the federal law, it is first determined whether the drug within Schedule I or II is a narcotic drug and then a penalty is imposed on this determination.

One very significant difference between the federal statute and the Virginia statute is that the latter does not provide that first offenders may have charges dismissed at the discretion of the court. Additionally, no provision is made for the criminal records of first offenders being expunged.

TABLE XLIX—VIRGINIA

Citation	Types of Drugs	Possession	Possession With Intent to Sell or Distribute	Sale or Distribution	Sale to a Minor
Va. Code Ann. Sec. 54-524.1 et seq. (Supp. 1970)	Schedule I: 42 specifically enumerated drugs; 17 opium derivatives; 13 hallucinogenic substances	*Except Marihuana* 1st: 1-10 yrs. in penitentiary or 1 yr. in county jail S: 2-20 yrs. in penitentiary or 1 yr. in county jail and $10,000	1st: NLT 1 yr. and NMT 40 yrs. and/or $25,000 S: 10 yrs. to life and/or $50,000	1st: NLT 1 yr. and NMT 40 yrs. and/or $25,000 S: 10 yrs. to life and/or $50,000	5-40 yrs. and/or $50,000
	Schedule II: Opium, cocaine, opiate, opium poppy and straw; 20 specific opiates	1st: 1-10 yrs. in penitentiary or 1 yr. in county jail S: 2-20 yrs. in penitentiary or 1 yr. in county jail and $10,000	1st: NLT 1 yr. and NMT 40 yrs. and/or $25,000 S: 10 to life and/or $50,000	1st: NLT 1 yr. and NMT 40 yrs. and/or $25,000 S: 10 to life and/or $50,000	5-40 yrs. and/or $50,000
	Schedule III: Amphetamine, Phenmetrazine,	Marihuana included: 1st: NMT 1 yr. and/or $1,000	1st: NLT 1 yr. and NMT 40 yrs. and/or $25,000	1st: NLT 1 yr. and NMT 40 yrs. and/or $25,000	5-40 yrs. and/or $50,000

Methylphenidate, 17 barbiturates	S: 2-20 yrs. in penitentiary or 1 yr. in county jail and $1,000	S: 10 to life and/or $50,000	S: 10 to life and/or $50,000	No specific provision
Schedule IV: Stimulants and Depressants exempted from Schedule III	NMT 1 yr. and/or $1,000	1st: NMT 1 yr. and/or $1,000 S: 1-5 yrs. in penitentiary or 1 yr. in county jail and/or $10,000	1st: NMT 1 yr. and/or $1,000 S: 1-5 yrs. in penitentiary or 1 yr. in county jail and/or $10,000	No specific provision
Schedule V: Compounds and preparations with small amounts of narcotics	NMT 1 yr. and/or $1,000	1st: NMT 1 yr. and/or $1,000 S: 1-5 yrs. in penitentiary or 1 yr. in county jail and/or $10,000	1st: NMT 1 yr. and/or $1,000 S: 1-5 yrs. in penitentiary or 1 yr. in county jail and/or $10,000	

1st = 1st offense.
2nd = 2nd offense.

3rd = 3rd offense.
S = Subsequent offense.

NMT = Not more than.
NLT = Not less than.

Washington: Wash. Rev. Code Ann., Sec. 69.33 et seq.
(Supp. 1969)

Washington has not combined drug abuse laws so that all controlled substances are embraced in one statute. The Uniform Narcotic Drug Act of Washington provides general penalty provisions for offenses involving narcotic drugs. Narcotic drugs under the Washington statute include coca, opium, drugs to which the federal laws relating to narcotic drugs now apply, and any drug found by the board of pharmacy to have addiction forming or addiction sustaining liability similar to morphine or cocaine. The statute specifically provides that narcotic drugs shall not include cannabis.

A separate statute regulates the unlawful manufacture, sale, distribution or possession of dangerous drugs. This statute does not attempt to define dangerous drugs but rather specifically provides that it is unlawful for a person, firm, or corporation to sell, give away, barter, exchange or distribute amytal, luminal, veronal, barbital, acid diethybarbituric, amphetamines, or marihuana. The use of the word "hallucinogenic" is avoided although the statute also makes it unlawful to sell, give away, barter, exchange or distribute dimethyltryptamine, lysergic acid, mescaline, peyote, psilocin, or their derivatives. Washington has not embarked on the road to classification of dangerous substances. Therefore, a drug is merely described in the statute which provides a penalty for unlawful manufacture, sale or possession.

The only determination, for purposes of imposing penalties, is whether the drug is a narcotic drug or a dangerous drug. This two dimensional approach to classification is much less complex than the classification involving five schedules of drugs used in the federal act and those states which have adopted the federal act.

West Virginia: W. Va. Code, Sec. 60-A (Supp. 1971)

West Virginia has enacted a Uniform Controlled Substances Act. This is similar to the *Federal Drug Abuse Prevention and Control Act of 1970*. The law, as enacted in West Virginia,

TABLE L—WASHINGTON

Citation	Type of Drug	General Penalty Provisions	Possession	Possession With Intent to Sell	Sale	Sale to a Minor
Wash. Rev. Code Ann. Sec. 69.33 et seq. (Supp. 1969) Narcotics	Narcotics: (Marihuana specifically excluded)	1st: 5-20 yrs. and/or NMT $10,000 2nd: 10-20 yrs. and/or NMT $10,000 3rd: 15-40 yrs. and/or NMT $25,000				1st and S: 20-40 yrs. and NMT $50,000
Wash. Rev. Code Ann. Sec. 69-40 et. seq. (Supp. 1969)	Dangerous Drugs: Amphetamines, Barbiturates, Hallucinogens, Marihuana Other Dangerous Drugs		Marihuana: 1st: NMT 6 mos. and/or NMT $500 2nd: NMT 1 yr. and/or NMT $1,000 S: NMT 10 yrs. and/or $10,000 NMT 10 yrs. and/or $10,000	Marihuana: 1st and S: 40 grams or more of Marihuana 3-10 yrs. and NMT $5,000 NMT 10 yrs. and/ or $10,000	Marihuana: 3-10 yrs. and NMT $5,000 3-10 yrs. and NMT $5,000	Marihuana: 1st and S: NMT 20 yrs. and NMT $50,000 NMT 20 yrs. and NMT $50,000

1st = 1st offense.
2nd = 2nd offense.

3rd = 3rd offense.
S = Subsequent offense.

NMT = Not more than.
NLT = Not less than.

TABLE LI—WEST VIRGINIA

Citation	Type of Drug	Possession	Possession With Intent to Sell	Distribution or Sale	Sale to a Minor
W. Va. Code Sec. 60-A (Supp. 1971)	Schedule I: 42 Opiates, 22 opium derivatives (heroin), 17 hallucinogens (marihuana)	1st: 90 days to 6 mos. and/or NMT $1,000 (except less than 15 grams of marihuana) S: Twice the penalty for 1st	Narcotic: 1st: 1-15 yrs. and/or NMT $25,000 Non-narcotic: 1st: 1-5 yrs. and/or NMT $15,000 S: Twice the penalty for 1st	Same as Possession with intent to sell	Narcotic: 1st: 2-30 yrs. and/or NMT $25,000 Non-narcotic: 1st: 2-10 yrs. and/or NMT $15,000 S: Twice the penalty for 1st
	Schedule II: Opium and opiates not in Schedule I. Opium poppy and poppy straw coca leaves (cocaine) 21 specific opiates	1st: 90 days to 6 mos. and/or NMT $1,000 S: Twice the penalty for 1st	Narcotic: 1st: 1-15 yrs. and/or NMT $25,000 Non-narcotic: 1st: 1-5 yrs. and/or NMT $15,000 S: Twice the penalty for 1st	Same as Possession with intent to sell	Narcotic: 1st: 2-30 yrs. and/or NMT $25,000 Non-narcotic: 1st: 2-10 yrs. and/or NMT $15,000 S: Twice the penalty for 1st

Schedule (Drugs)	Possession	Possession with intent to sell	Sale
Schedule III: Amphetamine, phe-metrazine, methamphet-amine, methylphenidate, 10 specific barbiturates, nalorphine preparations containing limited quantities of narcotics	1st: 90 days to 6 mos. and/or NMT $1,000. S: Twice the penalty for 1st	1st: 1-5 yrs. and/or NMT $15,000 S: Twice the penalty for 1st	Same as Possession with intent to sell	1st: 2-10 yrs. and/or NMT $15,000 S: Twice the penalty for 1st
Schedule IV: 11 drugs having a depressant effect on the central nervous system	1st: 90 days to 6 mos. and/or NMT $1,000. S: Twice the penalty for 1st	1st: 1-3 yrs. and/or NMT $10,000 S: Twice the penalty for 1st	Same as Possession with intent to sell	1st: 2-6 yrs. and/or NMT $10,000 S: Twice the penalty for 1st
Schedule V: Preparations containing small amounts of narcotic drugs	1st: 90 days to 6 mos. and/or NMT $1,000. S: Twice the penalty for 1st	1st: 6 mos. to 1 yr. and/or NMT $5,000 S: Twice the penalty for 1st	Same as Possession with intent to sell	1st: 1-2 yrs. and/or NMT $5,000 S: Twice the penalty for 1st

1st = 1st offense.
2nd = 2nd offense.

3rd = 3rd offense.
S   = Subsequent offense.

NMT = Not more than.
NLT = Not less than.

adopts five schedules similar to the schedules set forth in the federal law. The statutory criteria used to determine which of the five schedules a controlled substance will be placed under are identical to the criteria used within the federal act.

The West Virginia statute has adopted the further consideration of whether a drug within Schedule I or Schedule II is a narcotic or a non-narcotic substance before imposing a penalty. This is in contrast to many of the states which have not adopted the consideration embraced in the federal law of whether a drug is a narcotic or a non-narcotic substance within Schedule I or Schedule II. Since "narcotic drug" is defined as opium and opiate, opium poppy and poppy straw and coca leaves, offenses involving the hallucinogenic substances within Schedule I would not carry as harsh a penalty as the opium derivatives and opiates which come within the purview of Schedule I.

The rationale of classifying drugs within Schedule I or Schedule II, in view of the fact that the penalties imposed for offenses involving these substances are similar, is highly questionable. The West Virginia statute provides that the court may defer proceedings and place the offender on probation for first offenses involving the possession of controlled substances. This type of conditional discharge is discretionary in offenses involving all types of controlled substances except marihuana. In first offenses involving the possession of less than 15 grams of marihuana the conditional discharge is mandatory.

Wisconsin: Wis. Stat. Ann., Sec. 161-01 et seq. (Supp. 1970)

The drug abuse statutes in Wisconsin reflect the disparity which exists among the states' definitions of narcotics and dangerous drugs. The Wisconsin statute authorizes the Dangerous Substances Control Council to classify drugs as narcotic drugs or dangerous drugs. The narcotic drugs include the narrowest definition of all the states and the federal law. Wisconsin includes within the definition of narcotics opium, meperidine, Isonipecaine, methadone, methadol, alphaprodine, heptazone, ketobemidone and levorphan. The Dangerous Substances Control Council is empowered to add to the group of narcotic drugs any substance which is found to have addiction or psychological dependency potentialities similar to the narcotic drugs described

TABLE LII—WISCONSIN

Citation	Type of Drug	General Penalty Provisions	Possession	Possession With Intent to Sell	Sale	Sale to a Minor
Wis. Stat. Ann. Sec. 161.01 et seq. (Supp. 1970)	Narcotic: Opium, meperidine, Isonipecaine, methadone, methadol, alpha-prodine, heptazone, ketobemidone, levorphan (ex-cluding cocaine)	1st: 2-10 yrs. 2nd: 5-10 yrs. S: 10-20 yrs. (no parole or suspended sen-tence for 2nd or S offense)	Same as General Penalty Provisions	Same as General Penalty Provisions	Same as Gen-eral Penalty Provisions	1st: 3-25 yrs. 2nd: 20-life S: life imprison-ment
	Dangerous Drugs: Amphetamine, Barbiturates, Hallucinogens, Marihuana, co-caine		1st: NMT 1 yr. and/or $500 S: NMT 2 yrs. and/or $1,000	1st: NMT 5 yrs. and/or $5,000 2nd: NMT 10 yrs. and/or $10,000	1st: NMT 5 yrs. and/or $5,000 2nd: NMT 10 yrs. and/or $10,000	1st: NMT 15 yrs. 2nd: 30 yrs. to life S: life imprison-ment

1st = 1st offense.
2nd = 2nd offense.

3rd = 3rd offense.
S = Subsequent offense.

NMT = Not more than.
NLT = Not less than.

TABLE LIII—WYOMING

Citation	Type of Drug	Possession	Possession With Intent to Sell or Deliver	Sale or Delivery	Sale to a Minor
Wyo. Stat. Sec. 35.347-1 et seq. (Supp. 1971)	Schedule I: 42 opiates, 22 opium derivatives (heroin), 17 hallucinogenic substances (marihuana)	1st: NMT 6 mos. and NMT $1,000 2nd: NMT 6 mos. and NMT $1,000 S: 5 yrs. and/or $5,000	Narcotic: 1st: NMT 20 yrs. and/or NMT $25,000 S: NMT 40 yrs. and/or NMT $50,000 Non-narcotic: 1st: NMT 10 yrs. and/or $10,000 S: NMT 20 yrs. and/or $20,000	Same as Possession with Intent to Sell or Deliver	Twice the penalty authorized for ordinary sale
	Schedule II: Opium and opiate, opium poppy and poppy straw, coca leaves, 21 specific opiates	1st: NMT 6 mos. and NMT $1,000 2nd: NMT 6 mos. and NMT $1,000 S: 5 yrs. and/or $5,000	Narcotic: 1st: NMT 20 yrs. and/or NMT $25,000 S: NMT 40 yrs. and/or NMT $50,000 Non-narcotic: 1st: NMT 10 yrs. and/or $10,000 S: NMT 20 yrs. and/or $20,000	Same as Possession with Intent to Sell or Deliver	Twice the penalty authorized for ordinary sale

Schedule III: Amphetamine, phenmetrazine, methylphenidate, 10 specific barbiturates, preparations containing limited quantities of narcotic drugs	1st: NMT 6 mos. and NMT $1,000 2nd: NMT 6 mos. and NMT $1,000 S: 5 yrs. and/or $5,000	1st: NMT 10 yrs. and/or $10,000 S: NMT 20 yrs. and/or $20,000	Same as Possession with Intent to Sell or Deliver	Twice the penalty authorized for ordinary sale
Schedule IV: 11 specific substances having depressant effect on the central nervous system	1st: NMT 6 mos. and NMT $1,000 2nd: NMT 6 mos. and NMT $1,000 S: NMT 5 yrs. and/or $5,000	1st: NMT 2 yrs. and/or $2,500 or both S: NMT 4 yrs. and/or $5,000 or both	Same as Possession with Intent to Sell or Deliver	Twice the penalty authorized for ordinary sale
Schedule V: Compounds, mixtures or preparations containing limited quantities of narcotic drugs and also containing one or more non-narcotic active medicinal ingredients	1st: NMT 6 mos. and NMT $1,000 2nd: NMT 6 mos. and NMT $1,000 S: NMT 5 yrs. and/or $5,000	1st: NMT 1 yr. and/or $1,000 S: NMT 2 yrs. and/or $2,000	Same as Possession with Intent to Sell or Deliver	

1st = 1st offense.
2nd = 2nd offense.
3rd = 3rd offense.
S = Subsequent offense.
NMT = Not more than.
NLT = Not less than.

above. *It is most important to note that cocaine is not classified as a narcotic drug.* This gathers particular importance when considering the definitions of narcotic drugs in many other states which provide that substances containing addiction forming or addiction sustaining liabilities similar to opium or cocaine shall be classified as narcotics. In addition, the *Federal Drug Abuse Prevention and Control Act of 1970* classifies cocaine as a narcotic drug. Under the federal law whether a drug is a narcotic or non-narcotic is an important consideration when determining the sentence to be imposed. Cocaine being considered a narcotic by some states and the federal government but not a narcotic under Wisconsin law should well illustrate the need for concise criteria when dangerous drugs are defined and classified.

The second group of substances which are regulated by the drug abuse laws of Wisconsin are the dangerous drugs. The dangerous drugs include the amphetamines, barbiturates, hallucinogens, marihuana, coca leaves and cocaine, and ecgonine. As mentioned above, Wisconsin is the only jurisdiction which does not consider coca leaves, cocaine, or ecgonine as narcotic.

The Wisconsin statute provides for the conditional discharge of a first offender charged with the unlawful possession of a controlled substance if the offender complies with the terms and conditions of the probation.

Wyoming: Wyo. Stat., Sec. 35.347-1 et seq. (Supp. 1971)

Wyoming has enacted a Controlled Substances Act (1971). This act is similar to the *Federal Drug Abuse Prevention and Control Act of 1970.* The act provides five schedules of substances and the authorized penalties for offenses involving the controlled substances depends upon which schedule the drug is classified under.

It is significant to note that possession of *any* controlled substances is punishable by a maximum of six months in jail and a maximum fine of $1,000. In addition, a first offender may be placed on probation upon terms and conditions. This can be contrasted to the maximum penalty of life imprisonment that a first offender may receive under Texas law for unlawful possession of a narcotic drug.

CHAPTER V

PRESENT TRENDS REFLECTING INCREASED UTILIZATION OF THE UNIFORM CONTROLLED SUBSTANCES ACT

THE MATERIALS PRESENTED in the prior chapter do not reflect the most recent amendments to dangerous drug legislation in the United States. Recent legislative activity reflects increased utilization of the Uniform Controlled Substances Act.

The function of the Uniform Controlled Substances Act is to replace the Uniform Narcotic Drug Act which had been promulgated by the National Conference of Commissioners on Uniform State Laws in 1933 and the Model State Drug Abuse Control Act, dealing with hallucinogenic, stimulant and depressant drugs in 1966. It is significant to note that the adoption in 1966 of uniform State legislation regulating hallucinogenic, stimulant and depressant drugs was in response to the changing patterns of drug abuse. Drug abuse no longer focused exclusively on the more traditional types of abused drugs such as heroin and marihuana, but now extended to new types of drugs having a potential for abuse.

Federal legislation took cognizance of the broader patterns of drug abuse and the "Comprehensive Drug Abuse Prevention and Control Act of 1970" (discussed in prior chapters) focused on a wide range of dangerous drugs. The multitude of dangerous drugs were classified and scheduled into five basic schedules.

The modern federal legislation made it necessary for many states to amend existing legislation by adopting classifications similar to the federal approach. Ostensibly, classification of dangerous drugs is a definite and well entrenched trend in American dangerous drug legislation. The following States have adopted The Uniform Controlled Substances Act subsequent to the initial preparation of the charts and materials presented in the prior chapters.

169

Arkansas (Ark. Stat. Ann. Sec. 82-2601-82-2638).

California (Cal. Health and S. Code Sec. 11000-11651).

Hawaii (Hawaii Rev. Laws 329-1 et. seq.).

Idaho (Idaho Code Ann. 37-2701-37-2751).

Illinois (S.H.A. c56 1/2 Section 1100-1603).

Iowa (Iowa Code Ann. 204.101-204.602.)

Louisiana (La. Rev. Stat. Ann. Sec. 40.961-40.990).

Massachusetts (Mass. Gen. Laws Ann. c.94C Sec. 1 to 48).

Michigan (Mich. Comp. Laws Ann. Sec. 335.301-335.367)

Mississippi (Miss. Code Ann. 6831-51-6831-88).

Missouri (Mo. Rev. Stat. 195.010-195.320).

Nebraska (R.S. Supp. 1971, Sec. 28-4, 115 to 28-4, 142).

Nevada (Nev. Rev. Stat. 453.011 to 453.361).

New Jersey (N.J. Rev. Stat. Sec. 24:21-1 et seq.).

New York (McKinney's Public Health Law Sec. 330 et seq.).

North Dakota (N.D. Cent. Code Sec. 19-03.1).

Oklahoma (Okla. Stat. Ann. Sec. 2-101-2-610).

Pennsylvania (Pa. Stat. Sec. 780-101—780-144).

South Carolina (S.C. Code Ann. Sec. 32-1510.21—32-1510.69).

Washington (Wash. Rev. Code Ann. 69.50.101—69.50.608).

West Virginia (W. Va. Code Sec. 60-A).

Wisconsin (Wis. Stat. Ann. 161.001—161.62).

One of the primary purposes of the Uniform Controlled Substances Act was to create similarity between State and federal dangerous drug laws. The authors of the Act have stated that it was "designed to complement the new Federal narcotic and dangerous drug legislation and provide an interlocking trellis of Federal and State law to enable government at all levels to control more effectively the drug abuse problem."

An ultimate objective of the Act is to establish a comprehensive and coordinated effort by all states *to classify* all narcotic drugs, marihuana and dangerous drugs, into five schedules, each schedule having its own criteria for drug categorization.

The number of States having adopted the Uniform Act and the identical emphasis placed upon classification as in the "Comprehensive Drug Abuse Prevention and Control Act of 1970," reflects the growing importance of properly categorizing drugs at legislative and administrative levels.

Section 201 of the Act, as adopted by all States which have enacted a Uniform Controlled Substances Act, provides the criteria to be used in controlling and classifying drugs into five distinct schedules. These criteria are identical to the criteria provisions in the Federal Act, and basically provide that all controlled substances be classified in either Schedule I, II, III, IV, or V after considering the potential for abuse, known effect, harmfulness and level of accepted medical use of any particular controlled substance.

In essence, adoption of the Uniform Controlled Substances Act, which is a legislative prototype of federal dangerous drug laws, is an effort to establish a comprehensive, coordinated and codified legislative effort to prevent and control drug abuse. Of course, one of the disadvantages of the chief characteristic of uniformity is that many States will be combating varied patterns of drug abuse with a preconceived and classified type of legislation. This may prevent or hinder spontaneous or local legislative efforts in response to unique and varied drug abuse patterns. For example, one geographical location may experience abuse of a particular type of controlled substance to a lesser or greater degree than another geographical location.

The element of uniformity does not exist in regard to imposition of sentencing. The Act describes prohibited acts of unlawful manufacture and delivery of controlled substances or possession with intent to manufacture or deliver such substances. The offense and subsequent penalties are commensurate with the degree of particular danger to the public which the unlawful act presents. For example, unlawful manufacture and delivery of certain drugs in Schedule I purportedly presents more of a danger to the public than mere possession of a drug classified in Schedule V. However, it is significant to note that the Uniform Controlled Substances Act leaves the actual sentence length for any specific offense a matter of State determination. Therefore, the State, when adopting the Uniform Controlled Substances Act, will assign specific penalties to particular offenses.

It should be apparent at this point that the Scheduling of drugs is of primary importance and requires care and certainty when we consider the fact that sentences will pivot on these initial classification determinations.

The Act also contemplates vesting a judge with discretion to place a first offender on probation rather than sentencing him to prison in situations involving a first offense for simple possession of any controlled substance. However, the judge is not required to comply with this provision and may disregard the provision for a probated sentence. This poignant provision also provides for confidentiality of the defendant's criminal record upon satisfactory compliance with the terms and conditions of probation. This prevents a criminal record from stigmatizing the defendant in his future efforts.

It is significant to note that this provision permitting probation for the first offender is optional and many States have adopted the Act without adopting this particular section.

CHAPTER VI

THE ENFORCEMENT OF DANGEROUS DRUG LAWS: A CONSIDERATION OF EXCLUSIONARY RULES OF EVIDENCE AND THE DEFENSE OF ENTRAPMENT

DANGEROUS DRUG STATUTES and their ability to deter drug abuse, can only be evaluated within the framework of the entire legal system. This section will consider court decisions which have had a significant effect upon the enforcement of dangerous drug laws at state and federal levels.

A. Exclusionary Rules of Evidence: Legal Evolution of Mapp V. Ohio[1]

The Fourth Amendment of the United States Constitution provides that:

> The right of the people to be secure in their persons, houses, papers, and effects, against unreasonable searches and seizures, shall not be violated, and no warrants shall issue, but upon probable cause, supported by Oath or affirmation, and particularly describing the place to be searched, and the persons or things to be seized (U.S. Const. Amend. IV, Sec. 1).

Evidence obtained in violation of the Fourth Amendment first attained exclusionary status in federal prosecutions. In 1914, the Supreme Court of the United States, in the decision of *Weeks v. United States*,[2] held that in a federal prosecution the Fourth Amendment prevented the use of evidence which was obtained through an illegal search and seizure. In 1949, the United States Supreme Court was to decide whether the exclusionary rule of evidence which applied in federal prosecutions would be extended in state prosecutions. The issue presented to the court in *Wolf v. Colorado*[3] was whether violations of Fourth Amend-

---

[1] 367 U.S. 643 (1961).
[2] 232 U.S. 383 (1914).
[3] 338 U.S. 25 (1949).

ment rights would give rise to similar exclusionary rules of evidence at state levels. More specifically, the court considered whether the Fourth Amendment exclusionary rights would become obligatory upon the states by virtue of the due process clause of the Fourteenth Amendment. Justice Frankfurter, speaking for the court, held that the exclusionary rules of evidence would not be superimposed upon state prosecutions. The case adopted the rationale that although the practice of excluding illegally seized evidence may be an effective way of discouraging unreasonable searches, it would not be a task of the Supreme Court to design a remedy for those whose Fourth Amendment rights were violated. The court felt that the individual should rely upon other methods of being guaranteed his Fourth Amendment rights. Therefore, in a prosecution in a state court for a state crime, the Fourteenth Amendment would not be interpreted to forbid the admission of evidence obtained by an unreasonable search and seizure.

In 1961, in the case of *Mapp v. Ohio*[4] the Supreme Court overruled *Wolf v. Colorado*. In the Mapp case local police illegally obtained evidence from the home of Miss Mapp. Without a search warrant the police seized "obscene" literature and this was used as evidence at the trial of the accused. The defendant appealed the conviction arguing that the evidence obtained in violation of the search and seizure clause of the Fourth Amendment was improperly introduced as evidence in the state prosecution, and, therefore, was a denial of due process of law guaranteed by the Fourteenth Amendment. The Supreme Court overruled the decision of *Wolf v. Colorado* pivoting on the principle that state procedure did not compensate individuals whose Fourth Amendment rights had been violated. Civil actions against the offending officers were not successful in providing a remedy for a violation of these rights, and, therefore, the Fourth Amendment rights were merely form without substance. The civil suits were viewed by the court as being ineffective in controlling and preventing violations of Fourth Amendment rights. The court did not foresee any state control methods

---

[4] 367 U.S. 643 (1961).

which would act to discourage violations of these rights and, therefore, the court held that the constitutional right would be best protected by excluding all evidence which is obtained by an illegal search and seizure. Therefore, in a state prosecution evidence cannot be introduced if it was the product of an illegal search and seizure.

This has had a significant effect upon the enforcement of dangerous drug laws. The enforcement agencies are now required to delicately consider the suspect's Fourth Amendment rights to be free from unreasonable searches and seizures before seizing or searching a purported offender.

The *Mapp* decision has created a deeper respect for constitutional rights, but it has also presented obstacles to effective enforcement of drug laws. Law enforcement agents are now required to apprehend a suspected offender in a manner which will not provide the accused with the procedural means to challenge the legality of the contraband's apprehension and its admission in evidence. This has resulted in the need to train police carefully so that there are no violations of constitutional standards which will interfere with the effective prosecution of the accused.[5] These strict rules of evidence have also been noted as being responsible for the police testifying falsely of the circumstances surrounding the arrest of the accused.[6]

Some of the difficulties which are now presented to law enforcement agents are well illustrated by the case of *Sibron v. New York*.[7] Sibron was convicted for the unlawful possession of heroin. Before the trial he moved to suppress the evidence from being introduced arguing that the contraband was obtained as a result of an unlawful search of his person. This motion was denied and appeal was based upon this denial to suppress the evidence. The facts of the case as described at the hearing to suppress the evidence indicated that the arresting officer saw the accused with six or eight persons whom the police officer

---

[5] For an excellent article discussing the effects of Mapp v. Ohio on enforcement procedures; see *Effect of Mapp v. Ohio on Police Search and Seizure Practices in Narcotics Cases*, 4 Colum. J of Law and Soc Prob, 87 (1968).

[6] *Id.*

[7] 392 U.S. 40 (1967).

knew from past experience to be narcotic addicts. The officer testified that he did not overhear any of the conversation between the accused and the six or eight men and that he did not see anything passed among them. The arresting officer then observed the accused as he proceeded to a restaurant. Sibron, while in the restaurant, engaged in a conversation with three more known narcotic addicts. At this time the patrolman still did not hear any part of the conversation, and he did not observe the passage of any objects from one to the other. Then Sibron sat down and while having some pie and coffee the officer approached him and asked him to come outside. When outside the restaurant, the officer told Sibron, "You know what I am after." At this point, the arresting officer placed his hand in Sibron's pocket and removed several glassine envelopes containing heroin.

The Supreme Court of the United States reversed the decision of the New York Court of Appeals and held that this was an illegal search and seizure and the evidence would be inadmissible in any criminal proceedings. The court held that there was no basis for the inference that persons who talk to narcotic addicts are addicts themselves and that, therefore, there was no probable cause to search the person of the accused. The court held that there was no probable cause to arrest the defendant until after the search revealed packets of heroin.

A police officer is permitted to "stop and frisk" an individual and engage in "limited patting" in a search for dangerous weapons. The purpose of allowing this limited type of search is to allow the officer to discover the possession of a weapon which might be the instrument of an assault.[8] However, in the *Sibron* case the search was not for the purpose of protecting the officer by the possible discovery of a weapon having potential to harm the policeman and, therefore, the evidence was held to have been improperly introduced. The court held there was no reason for the officer to think that a crime was being committed and, therefore, the search was illegal.

As a result of the *Sibron* decision, many police now testify by

---

[8] 392 U.S. I (1967).

using the "dropsey" story. In these situations the arresting officer testifies that when he approached the defendant he noticed heroin, marihauana, or whatever the seized contraband may consist of, drop from the person of the defendant. The officer then testifies that he picked it up and after careful examination found that the material which was dropped was a drug not allowed to be possessed. Then the police officer testifies that he placed the defendant under arrest. The accused testifies that the policeman approached him on the street, searched him and placed him under arrest after discovering the dangerous drugs. Rosengart, in *The Bust Book for Lawyers*[9] states that:

> . . . everyone in the courthouse knows that most dropsey stories are fabrications but the judges accept the police officer's testimony because they believe the defendant to be actually guilty of the crime and they do not want him to escape on a technicality. Also many judges do not wish to offend the police and prosecutors by upsetting a process that has become systematized.[10]

There is endless case law which engages in a refined distinction of factual patterns for purposes of defining the limits of searches of persons and homes by law enforcement agents. It is important that the principles of law which are promulgated by these cases be carefully considered when evaluating the efficacy of any dangerous drug statutes.[11] If procedural obstacles detract from the vitality of the deterrent effect of dangerous drug laws then the procedural rules and the dangerous drug laws must be modified so that they may combine to complement each other rather than serve as antagonists. Dangerous drug laws and enforcement guidelines must be more effectively coordinated.

The following affidavit is filed to support a motion to suppress evidence which is obtained in violation of an accused's Fourth Amendment constitutional rights. If the court grants the motion, evidence obtained in violation of these constitutional provisions cannot be introduced in any subsequent judicial proceedings:

---

[9] Oliver Rosengart, *The Bust Book for Lawyers* (Nat'l Lawyers Guild 1970) .

[10] *Id.*, at 67.

[11] See, Hall, Kamisar, LaFave, and Israel, *Basic Criminal Procedure* (1969) .

CRIMINAL COURT OF THE CITY OF NEW YORK
COUNTY OF NEW YORK

People of the State of New York
—against—

AFFIDAVIT IN SUPPORT OF
MOTION TO SUPPRESS

. . . .

Defendant

. . . . , being duly sworn, deposes and says:
(Defendant's name)

1. That I am the defendant in the above mentioned case and I make this affidavit in support of a motion to suppress various items which I believe the prosecutor intends to introduce as evidence against me at my trial.

2. On the .... day of .... 1971, at approximately 1:00 a.m. I was walking on Lenox Avenue between 125th and 126th Streets, in the City, County and State of New York.

3. That I was stopped, my person was searched, and my effects were searched. More specifically, the shoulder bag which I was carrying was searched and confiscated. The arresting officer alleges to have found narcotic drugs in said shoulder bag.

4. That the arresting officer did not show me a search warrant. I did not consent to a search, and I believe that he did not have probable or reasonable cause to believe that a crime was being committed before he searched my person.

5. That the above related search and seizure was a violation of my rights under the Fourth Amendment of the Constitution of the United States.

WHEREFORE, I respectfully request that an order be made and entered suppressing the use of the aforementioned items in my trial in this case, and for such other and further relief as to this Court may seem just and proper under the circumstances.

Sworn to before me this
. . . . . . day of . . . ., 1972.

. . . .
(Name of defendant)

Where a search warrant has been obtained the offender often has opportunity to destroy drugs possessed illegally before the police obtain access to the premises to be searched. This has resulted in the passage of "no-knock" statutes. The federal drug law[12] provides that where a search warrant is issued for offenses involving controlled substances certain circumstances may require a quick entry to the premises. The Federal Drug Abuse Prevention and Control Act of 1970 provides that a warrant will be issued where probable cause exists for believing that there are offenses involving controlled substances. The statute further provides that:

> Any officer authorized to execute a search warrant relating to offenses involving controlled substances the penalty for which is imprisonment for more than one year may, without notice of his authority and purpose, break open an outer or inner door or window of a building, or any part of the building, or anything therein, if the judge or United States magistrate issuing the warrant (1) is satisfied that there is probable cause to believe that (a) the property sought may, and if such notice is given, will be easily and quickly destroyed or disposed of, or (b) the giving of such notice will immediately endanger the life or safety of the executing officer or another person, and (2) has included in the warrant a direction that the officer executing it shall not be required to give such notice. Any officer acting under such warrant, shall as soon as practicable after entering the premises, identify himself and give the reasons and authority for his entrance upon the premises.[13]

The "no-knock" provisions described above have been constitutionally criticized as being violative of Fourth and Fifth Amendment guarantees.[14] It has been stated that this provision does not assure that the people will be "secure in their persons, houses, papers and effects against unreasonable searches and seizures." Some have stated that, "these objectionable provisions are seen to be the surveyor's slash through the majestic wilderness of privacy which may become the road that will despoil it."[15] It is, therefore, apparent that even when efforts are made to minimize the administrative obstructions to the effective enforcement of dangerous drug laws there is strong opposition

---

[12] 21 U.S.C.A. 801 *et seq.* (1970).
[13] 21 U.S.C.A. 879(b) (1970).
[14] 1970 U.S. Code Cong. and Adm. News, pp. 5715-5717.
[15] *Id.*, at 5717.

from those forces favoring a strict interpretation of constitutional guarantees.

B. The Entrapment Defense

The defense of entrapment is often introduced in dangerous drug cases. These cases and the peculiar problems they present to law enforcement agents often create the necessity to resort to entrapment techniques. In most instances violations of dangerous drug laws involve secret and consensual transactions and detection is most difficult unless the enforcement agents employ inducement techniques.

Entrapment is often a detection technique employed by police to gather evidence of offenses which are usually committed with a willing victim who will not cooperate with enforcement agents. In these situations the police are said to "encourage" the purported offender to commit the offense in their presence.

An illustration of the need for entrapment is reflected in a situation where it becomes the objective of enforcement agents to obtain a conviction for the illegal sale of controlled substances. There may be substantial evidence that a suspect is in possession of large amounts of controlled substances and known addicts may be observed entering and leaving the suspect's home. This may be sufficient "probable cause" for the arrest of the offender and a subsequent search of his home may uncover evidence to convict the offender of possession of controlled substances. However, this evidence will not be sufficient to prove the sale of controlled substances. It is apparent that additional methods must often be employed to gather evidence which will carry the suspected criminal activities from the suspicion stage to an accusatorial stage based on substantial evidence.[16] The alternative methods employed often involve encouragement which is so persistent that an otherwise innocent person may succumb to the encouragement to commit a crime only because of the police inducement. Police inducement used as a detection technique, has

---

[16] See, Rotenberg, *The Police Detection Practice of Encouragement,* 49 Va. L. Rev. 871, 874-879 (1963).

clashed with judicial standards of an acceptable administration of justice.

1. *Judicial Standards Impose Limitations on Police Inducement*

The courts have defined entrapment as "the conception and planning of an offense by an officer and his procurement of its commission by one who would not have perpetrated it except for the trickery, persuasion or fraud of the officer."[17] The courts have held that the word "officer" includes police officers, law enforcement agents, and private citizens cooperating with police as informers.[18] In a case where the defense of entrapment is introduced it is generally argued that the intention that the crime be committed had its origin with the police, and in the absence of their inducement the crime would not have occurred. The defense is successfully introduced where it is evident that if entrapment was not used as a prosecutorial instrument the accused would have obeyed the law. *Sherman v. United States*[19] illustrates judicial recognition of the entrapment defense. The facts indicated that Kalchinian, a government informer, and Sherman were being treated to cure drug addiction. Kalchinian asked Sherman to obtain narcotics for him. The evidence indicated that at first Sherman resisted but after repeated requests he supplied Kalchinian with narcotics. The trial court submitted the issue of entrapment to the jury but the jury felt there was no entrapment and consequently found the defendant guilty of illegally selling narcotic drugs.

The United States Supreme Court reversed, finding entrapment as a matter of law.[20] The Supreme Court noted that there was no evidence that the petitioner was engaged in the trade of

---

[17] Sorrels v. United States, 287 U.S. 435, 454 (1932).

[18] See, Note, *Entrapment,* 73 Harv. L. Rev. 1333, 1340-1341 (1960).

[19] 356 U.S. 369 (1958).

[20] It is important to note that Kalchinian, the government informer, was cooperating with the Federal Bureau of Narcotics in hope of obtaining a suspended sentence for his own conviction of illegally selling narcotics. He later received a suspended sentence in response to a statement by the United States Attorney to the Judge that he had been cooperative with the Government.

selling narcotic drugs. The court emphasized the following facts to substantiate the defense of entrapment: (1) When Sherman's apartment was searched after his arrest, there were no narcotics found. (2) There was no significant evidence that Sherman made a profit on any sale to the government agent. (3) There was evidence that the accused resisted the request of the informer.[21] The court held that it was clear that Sherman was induced by the government's agent to commit the offense. The informer's testimony indicated that although he knew the petitioner was undergoing a cure for narcotic addiction, he nonetheless sought to persuade the petitioner to obtain narcotics for him. The testimony further indicated that one request for the narcotic drugs was not enough because the accused first refused and evaded the demands and hesitated to comply with the request.[22]

Sherman v. United States failed to clarify three important dimensions of the law of entrapment. (1) The court failed to clearly express the legal justification for the doctrine. (2) There was no decision of whether the issue of entrapment was to be decided by the judge or the jury. (3) The court did not decide whether evidence of the defendant's prior conduct should be admissible.[23]

Generally, the issue of entrapment is decided by the jury unless the evidence is so clear and convincing that entrapment is established as a matter of law.[24]

Legal justification for the defense of entrapment has rested on the foundation that the acts of a person did not come within purview of the prohibited conduct as described by statute, "because it cannot be supposed that Congress intended that the letter of its enactment should be used to support such a gross perversion of its purpose."[25] However, some United States Supreme

---

[21] Sherman v. United States, 356 U.S. 369, 371 (1958).

[22] *Id.*

[23] For an excellent discussion of these issues see, Cowen, *The Entrapment Doctrine in the Federal Courts and Some State Court Comparisons,* 49 J. Crim. L. C. & P.S. 447 (1959).

[24] See, Note, *The Defense of Entrapment in California,* 19 Hastings Law Journal 825 (1968).

[25] Sorrels v. United States, 287 U.S. 435, at 452 (1932).

Court Justices have stated that the legal theory of the defense of entrapment rests upon the accepted jurisdiction of the courts to mold proper standards for enforcement of the federal criminal law in the federal courts in situations involving an absence of congressional regulatory legislation.[26]

The issue of whether a defendant's prior criminal conduct is admissible as evidence to prove the accused was not induced to commit the crime has not been clearly decided by the courts. The types of prior offenses admitted into evidence to illustrate the criminal propensities of an accused for purposes of controverting the defense of entrapment vary among the courts.[27] In most instances each case is judged on its own peculiar facts and circumstances and there is a lack of definitive judicial guidelines. The guidelines established in the *Sorrels*[28] decision and adopted in the *Sherman*[29] decision merely provide that when the defense of entrapment is introduced the prosecution may defeat the claim of entrapment by showing the readiness or predisposition of the accused to commit the offense. As stated in *Sherman v. United States*[30]

> . . . at trial the accused may examine the conduct of the government agent; and *on the other hand the accused will be subjected to an "appropriate and searching inquiry into his own conduct and predisposition" as bearing on his claim of innocence.* [emphasis added]

This should illustrate that the introduction of the defense of entrapment can lead to concentrated focus on the prior conduct of the defendant instead of the behavioral inducement factors on the part of the government agent. *Sherman v. United States*[31] failed to define the scope of inquiry an accused may be subjected to when the prosecution attempts to illustrate the crim-

---

[26] Sherman v. United States, 356 U.S. 369 at 380-81 (1958) (concurring opinion).

[27] Hansford v. United States, 303 F. 2d 219 (D.C. Cir. 1962) illustrates the need for definitive judicial guidelines when delicate issues of evidence arise in trials where the defense of entrapment is introduced.

[28] *Supra*, note 17.

[29] *Supra*, note 26.

[30] *Supra*, note 26, at 373.

[31] *Supra*, note 26.

inal propensities of the accused.[32] Therefore, it is not clear whether hearsay evidence could be introduced by prosecution to show the readiness of an accused to commit the offense charged or if prior records of arrests or indictments, even if resulting in acquittals, would be admissible.[33] The courts have not decided whether the offense introduced to illustrate the prior criminal propensities of an accused must be sufficiently related to the crime for which the defense of entrapment is introduced.

2. Establishing Guidelines to be Used in Determining the Validity of Entrapment Defenses

Referring to the doctrine of entrapment, Justice Frankfurter stated that "Human nature is weak enough and sufficiently beset by temptations without government adding to them by generating crime."[34] Therefore, Justice Frankfurter suggested that the courts consider the setting in which the inducement took place, the nature of the crime involved, the secrecy and difficulty of detecting the crime involved, and the manner in which the particular criminal business is conducted.[35] There is also a significant contention that the issue of entrapment be considered by the court instead of the jury. It is argued that "although the jury verdict may settle the issue of entrapment in a particular case" there are no significant guidelines for the future. The court, the argument holds, "through the gradual evolution of explicit standards in accumulated precedents, can do this with the degree of certainty that the wise administration of criminal justice demands."[36]

In the concurring opinion of *Sherman*, Justice Frankfurter noted that "a statute which prohibits the sale of narcotics is as silent on the questions of entrapment as it is on the admissibility of illegally obtained evidence."[37] Statutes are enacted on the

---

[32] In Hansford v. United States, 303 F. 2d 219 (D.C. Cir. 1962) it was held to be reversible error for the trial court to allow the prosecution to introduce *hearsay evidence* which was highly prejudicial.

[33] *Id.*

[34] Sherman v. United States, *Supra,* note 26, at 384 (concurring opinion).

[35] *Id.*

[36] *Id.,* at 385.

[37] *Supra,* note 26, at 381 (concurring opinion).

basis of "certain presuppositions concerning the established legal order and the role of the courts within that system in formulating standards for the administration of criminal justice when Congress, itself, has not specifically legislated to that end."[38]

Effective enforcement of dangerous drug laws requires a carefully coordinated effort between legislatures and the courts. The scope and limits of the entrapment defense should be clearly defined so that specific statutes can be enforced effectively within the mandates of an "antecedent legal system."

---

[38] *Id.*

CHAPTER VII

CIVIL COMMITMENT OF DRUG ADDICTS

> It is unlikely that any State at this moment in history would attempt to make it a criminal offense for a person to be mentally ill, or a leper, or be afflicted with a venereal disease. A State might determine that the victims of these and other human afflictions be dealt with by compulsory treatment, involving quarantine, confinement, or sequestration. But, in the light of contemporary human knowledge, a law which made a criminal offense of such a disease (narcotic addiction) would doubtless be universally thought to be an infliction of cruel and unusual punishment in violation of the Eighth and Fourteenth Amendments. Justice Douglas, *Robinson* v. *California* 370 U.S. 660, 666 (concurring opinion).

Robinson v. California[1] provided that it is a violation of the Eighth and Fourteenth Amendments of the Constitution for a State to consider and punish the status of narcotic addiction as a crime. However, the *Robinson* decision did suggest that:

> In the interest of discouraging the violation of such laws or in the interest of the general health or welfare of its inhabitants, a State might establish a program of compulsory treatment for those addicted to narcotics. Such a program of treatment might require involuntary periods of confinement.[2]

Programs of compulsory treatment, often referred to as *civil commitment,* involve confinement in a drug abuse rehabilitation center and subsequent treatment under supervision similar to parole. The objectives of the rehabilitation program are to have the drug addict[3] overcome physical dependence of narcotic drugs by providing varied therapeutic techniques which will as-

---

[1] 370 U.S. 660 (1962).

[2] *Id.* at 664-65.

[3] Subsection 2901 (a) of Federal Title 28 defines an "addict" as: ". . . any individual who habitually uses any narcotic drug . . . so as to endanger the public morals, health, safety, or welfare, or who is so far addicted to the use of such narcotic drugs as to have lost the power of self-control with reference to his addiction."

sist the addict in conquering the psychological need for narcotic drugs.

There have been constitutional objections to the involuntary civil commitment of addicts who have not been arrested or sentenced for any criminal offense.[4] However, the majority of civil commitments involve addicts who are given a choice of volunteering for a rehabilitation program instead of facing prosecution for a particular offense.

Federal Law of Civil Commitment and Rehabilitation of Narcotic Addicts[5]

The United States district court is vested with the discretionary authority to hold a criminal charge in abeyance if the court believes the individual is an addict and he is likely to be responsive to rehabilitative treatment. If the accused elects civil commitment in lieu of facing criminal charges he cannot withdraw from the treatment which follows and confinement may last for a maximum of thirty-six months. Additional supervised aftercare treatment may also be demanded.[6]

The individual has only five days from the time he is advised of the option to decide whether to volunteer for civil commitment or face the criminal charges which will be held in abeyance.[7] The maximum five-day period which is given to make the election often prevents the defendant from filing pretrial motions before deciding to volunteer for a rehabilitation program and therefore he may be forced to forego a valid defense of the criminal charges.[8]

If the defendant chooses civil commitment he is examined by

---

[4] *See* generally, criticisms of involuntary commitment of addicts who are not criminals: Aronowitz, *Civil Commitment of Narcotic Addicts*, 67 Colum. L. Rev. 405 (1967). Comment, *Civil Commitment of Narcotic Addicts*, 76 Yale L.J. 1160 (1967).

[5] 28 U.S.C. 2901 et seq.

[6] 28 U.S.C. 2902(a).

[7] *Id.*

[8] *See*, Aronowitz, *Civil Commitment of Narcotic Addicts and Sentencing for Narcotic Drug Offenses*, published as Appendix D to *Task Force Report: Narcotics and Drug Abuse*, p. 148 (G.P.O. 1967).

the Surgeon General and it is determined whether the defendant is an addict. If the Surgeon General's report does not state the accused is an addict who might be rehabilitated through treatment, the defendant must then answer the abeyant criminal charge.[9] If the report indicates the defendant is an addict and is likely to be rehabilitated through treatment, the court commits the defendant to the custody of the Surgeon General if adequate facilities and personnel for treatment are available.[10]

When an individual is committed to the custody of the Surgeon General the criminal charge is continued against him without final disposition. If the accused completes the rehabilitation program satisfactorily the charge against him is dismissed and he is released. If the accused does not complete the rehabilitation program satisfactorily the commitment is terminated and the criminal proceeding is resumed.[11] The defendant committed to institutional custody is subject to penalties if he escapes or attempts to escape.[12]

An individual is not eligible for civil comitment if he is charged with: (1) A crime of violence; or (2) Unlawful importing, selling, or conspiring to import or sell a narcotic drug.[13] The election of commitment is not available to a defendant against whom there is pending a prior charge of a felony or who is on probation. If on probation, the person authorized to require his return to custody might consent to the commitment and in this instance the election is made available to the accused.[14]

The election is not available to an individual who has been convicted of a felony on two or more occasions[15] or to an individual who has been civilly committed under federal law, the code of District of Columbia, or any state proceeding because of narcotic addiction on three or more occasions.[16]

If an abeyant criminal proceeding against an individual is re-

---

[9] 28 U.S.C.A. 2902(b).
[10] Id.
[11] 28 U.S.C.A. 2902(c).
[12] 28 U.S.C. 2902(d).
[13] 28 U.S.C. 2901(g)(1-2).
[14] 28 U.S.C. 2901(g)(3).
[15] 28 U.S.C. 2901(g)(4).
[16] 28 U.S.C. 2901(g)(5).

sumed because of the accused's noncompliance with the provisions of the rehabilitation program he receives credit for the time spent in the institutional custody of the Surgeon General.[17] The determination of narcotic addiction and the results of tests cannot be used against the accused except that the fact that he is a narcotic addict may be elicited on his cross-examination as bearing on his credibility as a witness.[18]

If the court does not offer a defendant an election of civil commitment there is no appellate review of his determination.[19]

State civil commitment programs resemble the federal law but they are somewhat distinguishable. For example, federal law excludes individuals from rehabilitation programs if they have been convicted of two or more felonies but New York law excludes anyone with a prior felony record.[20] The federal law does not grant civil commitment in situations involving offenders who have been civilly committed on three prior occasions but the law of New York provides that civil commitment will not prevail if there has been *any* prior certification to the care and custody of the commission.[21] This indicates that addicts in need of the rehabilitation program most are often discouraged and prevented from pursuing institutionalized/rehabilitative programs.

---

[17] 28 U.S.C. 2903(d).
[18] 28 U.S.C. 2904.
[19] 28 U.S.C. 2906.
[20] N.Y. Ment. Hyg. Law Sec. 210(2)(b).
[21] N.Y. Ment. Hyg. Law Sec. 210(2)(c).

INDEX

A

Adams, Roger, 14
Addicts
  civil commitment of, 9, 186-189
    federal law as to, 187-189
    state programs as to, 189
  compulsory treatment of, 186
  crime of being an addict, 136, 138
  involuntary commitment of, consti-
    tutionality of, 187
Alabama
  amphetamines, 40
  barbiturates, 40
  disparity in punishment, 8
  hallucinogens, 41
  marihuana, 38
  sale to minor of drugs, penalty for, 7
  state drug abuse law, 38-42
  statutory chart, 39
Alaska
  depressants, 42
  drugs, 42
  hallucinogens, 5, 42
  marihuana, 42
  sale to minor, penalty for, 7
  statutory chart, 43
  stimulant drug, 42
Amphetamines, 8, 15
  (see also specific state)
  classification and definition of, 4, 6
Amytal, 16
Arizona
  amphetamines, 47
  barbiturates, 47
  hallucinogens, 47
  marihuana, classification of, 11, 44
  minor, sale to, 46
  statutory chart, 45
  Uniform Narcotic Drug Act, 44
Arkansas
  amphetamines, 50
  barbiturates, 50
  marihuana, 48

statutory chart, 49
Uniform Narcotic Drug Act, 48

B

Barbital, 16
Barbiturates, 8, 15, 16
  (see also specific state)
  addiction potential of, 16
  classification and definition of, 4, 6
  danger of, 16
  medical use of, 16
Benzedrine, 15
Bhang, 13
  (see also Marihuana)

C

California, 50-52, 138
  marihuana, 50
  peyote, 50
Cannabinol, 13
Cannabis indica, 13
  (see also Marihuana)
Cannabis sativa, 13
  (see also Marihuana)
Charas, 13
  (see also Marihuana)
Chlordiazeoxide, 17
Classification
  (see also specific state)
  adoption of federal law by states,
    169-172
  comparison of legislative definitions
    and pharmacological classifica-
    tions, 4-7
  uniformity, lack of, 6
Coca plant, 12-13
Cocaine, 12-13
  addiction potential of, 13
  effect of, 13
  narcotic drug or dangerous drug?,
    168
  penalty, effect on, 5
  source of, 13

191

Codeine, 12
Colorado, 52
  marihuana, 52
  peyote, 53
  statutory chart, 53
Connecticut, 52, 55
  marihuana, 55
  statutory chart, 54
Constitution
  effect on dangerous drug laws, 9
  (*see also* Evidence)
Controlled drugs, 11
Cruel and unusual punishment, addiction, crime of, 138, 186

D

Dangerous drugs, 14, 15
  cocaine as, 5
  legislative classification of, 4-7
Death sentence, sale of minor of drug, 8
Definitions, comparisons of legislative definitions and classifications, 4-7
Delaware, 55-62
  amphetamines, 59
  barbiturates, 59
  comparison with other states, 64
  narcotic drugs, 55
  progressive nature of statutes of, 55, 59, 62
  sales, policy as to, 58
  statutory chart, 56
Depressant, 16-17
  (*see also* Barbiturates)
  heroin as, 12
Dexedrine, 15
District of Columbia, 62, 64
  statutory chart, 61
Drug abuse, changing nature of, 169

E

Enforcement, 173-185
Entrapment, 9, 180-185
  critique of, 180
  definition, 181
  Hansford v. U.S., 183n
  hearsay, 184
  judicial standards as to, 181-184
  need for, 180

Sherman v. U.S., 181, 182
Sorrels v. U.S., 182n
  validity of defense, 184
Equanil, 17
Evidence
  affidavit of motion to suppress, 178
  "dropsey," 177
  enforcement problems, 175
  exclusionary rules of, 9, 173-180
  Mapp v. Ohio, 173 *et seq.*
  no-knock statutes, 179
  search and seizure, 173 *et seq.*
  search warrant, 178
  Sibron v. N.Y., 175 *et seq.*
  stop and frisk, 176
  Weeks v. U.S., 173
  Wolf v. Colorado, 173 *et seq.*

F

Federal Drug Abuse Prevention and Control Act of 1970, 7
  explanation of, 171
  organized crime and, 8
  rationale for, 169
  schedules of, 171
  search warrants and, 179
  state statutes similar to, 48, 86, 92, 103, 110, 117, 129, 144, 151, 157, 160, 164, 168
  states adopting, 7
First offender, 8, 111, 145, 164, 168, 172
  (*see also* specific state)
  Uniform Controlled Substances Act, 9, 172
Florida, 62-64
  paraphernalia and, 64
  statutory chart, 62
  Uniform Narcotic Drug Act, 62
Fourth Amendment (*see* Evidence)
Frankfurter, J., 174, 184

G

Georgia, 64-67
  amphetamines, 66, 67
  barbiturates, 66
  dangerous drugs, 64
  Drug Abuse Control Act, 66
  LSD, 5, 67

marihuana, 66
minor, sale of drug to, 8
narcotic drugs, 66
statutory chart, 65
Uniform Narcotic Drug Act, 66

H

Hallucinogens, 15, 17, 18
    (*see also* specific state)
    legislative classification of, 4-7
    marihuana classified as, 4, 6
    penalty as to
        classification as narcotic, hallucino-
            gen, or stimulant and depres-
            sant, 5
        table, 6
    prohibition of sale or possession only,
        5, 6
Hard drugs, 5
Hashish, 13
    (*see also* Marihuana)
Hawaii, 67-69, 70
    minors, 70
    statutory chart, 68
Heroin, 12
    smuggling, 12

I

Idaho, 7, 70
    statutory chart, 69
    Uniform Controlled Substances Act,
        70
Illinois, 70-72
    Drug Abuse Control Act, 72
    marihuana, 72
    statutory chart, 71
Indiana, 73-76
    common nuisance provision, 75
    Dangerous Drug Act, 73
    minor, sale of drug to, 8
    non-narcotic drugs, classification of,
        5-6
    statutory chart, 74
Iowa, 76-78
    disparity in punishment, 8, 78
    marihuana, 76
    minors, 78
    statutory chart, 77
    Uniform Narcotic Drug Act, 76

K

Kansas, 78-83
    marihuana, 79, 82
    minor, sale of drug to, 8
    ordinances regulating drugs, 79
    physicians and pharmacists, 78-79
    statutory chart, 80-81
    Uniform Narcotic Drug Act, 78, 82
Kentucky, 83-86
    progressive approach of, 85
    rehabilitation and, 85-86
    statutory chart, 84
    strict penalties, 83
    Uniform Narcotic Drug Act, 83

L

Legend drugs, 149
Legislation
    (*see* Federal Drug Abuse Prevention
        and Control Act, *see also* spe-
        cific state)
    comparative study, need for, 3
    deficiency of legislators in knowledge
        of drugs, 6
Librium, 17
Louisiana, 7, 86-90
    marihuana, 90
    statutory chart, 87
    Uniform Controlled Dangerous Sub-
        stances Law, 86
    Uniform Narcotic Drug Law, 86
LSD (*see* Hallucinogens)

M

Maine, 90-92
    marihuana, 90, 91
    minor, 92
    statutory chart, 91
Marihuana
    (*see also* specific state)
    classification of, 4, 6
        hallucinogenic substance, as a, 4,
            6, 14
        narcotic drug, as a, 4, 14
        penalty, effect on, 4-5
    classified as narcotic, 11
    derivation of, 13
    disparity of sentencing for possession
        of, 8

grows anywhere, 13
history in United States, 13-14
physical effects of, 14
psychological effect of, 14
sexual effect of, 14
Maryland, 7, 92-93
  Controlled Dangerous Substance Act, 92
  marihuana, 93
  record, expunging of, 93
  statutory chart, 94-95
  Uniform Controlled Substances Act, 9
Massachusetts, 93-98
  hallucinogen, 5
  marihuana, 97
  narcotic includes hallucinogens, 97
  paraphernalia, penalty for, 98
  statutory chart, 96
  Uniform Narcotic Drug Law, 97
Meprobamate, 17
Mescaline (*see* Hallucinogens)
Methedrine, 15
Michigan, 98-100
  marihuana, 98
  privileged communications as to drugs, 100
  Uniform Narcotic Drug Act, 98
Middle East, 12
Miltown, 17
Minnesota, 100-103
  discretion of court in sentencing, 100
  marihuana, 102
  prohibited drugs, 102
  statutory chart, 101
  Steeves v. State, 102
  Uniform Narcotic Drug Act, 100
Minors
  (*see also* specific state)
  first offender, 8
  penalties provided for sale to, 7-8
Mississippi, 7, 103-106
  statutory chart, 104
  Uniform Controlled Substances Act, 103
Missouri, 106-108
  definitions, arbitrariness of, 106, 108
  sale to minor of drugs, penalty for, 7, 106
  statutory chart, 107

Montana, 108-111
  Dangerous Drug Act, 108
  marihuana, 110
  penalties and classification, 108
  State v. Dunn, 110
  Statutory Drug Act, 108
Morphine, 11-12

N

Narcotics
  (*see also* specific state)
  classes of, 11-14
  cocaine as, 5
  legislative classification of, 4-7
  marihuana classified as, 11
National Conference of Commissioners on Uniform State Laws, 169
Nebraska, 111-113
  marihuana, first offense for possession of, 8, 111
  statutory chart, 112
Nevada, 113-115
  dangerous drugs, 113
  prescriptions, 113
  statutory chart, 114
  Uniform Narcotic Drug Act, 113
New Hampshire, 115-117
  Controlled Drug Act, 115
  definitions are excellent, 117
  statutory chart, 116
New Jersey, 7, 117-121, 124
  Controlled Dangerous Substances Act, 117
  expunging record, 121
  marihuana, 120
  minors, 120
  progressive provisions of, 120
  statutory chart, 118-119
  Uniform Controlled Substances Act, 9
New Mexico, 121-124
  Drug and Cosmetic Act, 121
  expunging record, 124
  Marihuana Act of 1971, 124
  Narcotic Drug Act, 124
  statutory chart, 122-123
New York, 100, 125
  civil commitment of addicts, 189
  marihuana, 125
  statutory chart, 126-127

North Carolina, 125, 129
  broad nature of legislation, 125
  marihuana, 129
  statutory chart, 128
North Dakota, 7, 129-132
  statutory chart, 130-131
  Uniform Controlled Substances Act, 9, 129

O

Ohio, 132-134
  carnal knowledge and drug law, 134
  marihuana, 134
  statutory chart, 133
Oklahoma, 134-136, 138
  addict, crime of being an, 136
  marihuana, 134
  questionable definitions in law, 136
  sale to minor of drugs, penalty for, 7
  statutory chart, 135
Opiates
  (*see also* Narcotics)
  description of, 11-12
  medical value of, 11-12
Opium, 11
  countries producing, 12
Oregon, 137, 138
  discretion of court, 138
  statutory chart, 137
Organized crime, federal drug law and, 8

P

Paraphernalia, drug, 64, 98
Penalties
  (*see also* specific state)
  classification of drugs for, 4, 7
  disparities in punishment, 8
  jurisdictional comparisons, 7-10
  marihuana, status of as to, 4-6
  minor, sale to, 7-8
Pentothal, 16
Pep pills, 15
Peyote, 50, 53
  (*see also* Hallucinogens)
Pharmacological classifications compared with legislative definitions, 4-7
Privileged communications, 100

Psilocybin (*see* Hallucinogens)
Pyrahexyl, 14

R

Rehabilitation
  civil commitment and, 186
  federal law as to, 187
  state effort in, 85-86
Rhode Island, 140-142
  Barbiturates and Central Nervous System Stimulant Act, 140
  hallucinogens, 5
  harshness of penalties, 140
  narcotics included with hallucinogens, 140
  statutory chart, 141
  Uniform Narcotic Drug Act, 140
Robinson v. California, 136, 186
Rosengart, Oliver, 177

S

South Carolina, 142-144
  confusion in law, 142
  discretion of court, 144
  hallucinogens, 5
  punishment not harsh, 144
  statutory chart, 143
South Dakota, 7
  Drugs and Substances Control Act, 144
  first offenders, 145
  Uniform Controlled Substances Act, 144
State drug abuse laws, 38-168
Stimulants, 15, 16
  (*see* Amphetamines)
  addiction effect of, 15
  medical aspects of, 15
Suicide, 17

T

Tennessee, 145-149
  hallucinogens not mentioned in act, 149
  harshness of penalty, 149
  legend drugs, 149
  marihuana, 149
  statutory chart, 146-148
Texas, 149-151
  classification system faulty, 149, 151

hallucinogens, 149-151
harshness of penalties, 150-151, 157
marihuana, offense for possession of,
8
sale to minor of drugs, penalty for, 7
statutory chart, 150
Truth serum, 16

U

Uniform Controlled Substances Act, 9
(*see also* specific state)
confidentiality of record, 172
discretion of court, 172
first offender, 172
increased use of, 169-172
local experimentation, can curb, 171
purpose is to standardize federal and
state laws, 170
states adopting, 170
Uniform Narcotic Drug Act
(*see also* specific state)
replaced by Uniform Controlled Substances Act, 169
Utah, 7, 151-153, 156
Controlled Substances Act, 151
marihuana, 151
statutory chart, 152-153

V

Vermont, 156-157
marihuana, 156

rational provisions of, 156
sale of regulated drugs, 157
statutory chart, 154-155
Virginia, 7, 157
Drug Control Act, 157
statutory chart, 158-159
Uniform Controlled Substances Act,
9

W

Washington, 160-161
classification two dimensional, 160
statutory chart, 161
Uniform Narcotic Drug Act, 160
West Virginia, 7, 160, 164
critique of classification scheme, 164
first offense, 164
statutory chart, 162-163
Uniform Controlled Substances Act,
9, 160
Wisconsin, 164-168
cocaine, 5, 168
Dangerous Substances Control Council, 164
first offender, 168
statutory chart, 165
Wyoming, 7, 168
Controlled Substances Act, 168
first offender, 168
statutory chart, 166, 167